THE ART OF DELEGATING

A TutorText

The Art of

PUBLISHED BY

DOUBLEDAY & COMPANY, INC., GARDEN CITY, N.Y.

1965

DELEGATING

by Neely D. Gardner
and John N. Davis

PREPARED UNDER THE DIRECTION OF

EDUCATIONAL SCIENCE DIVISION

U. S. Industries, Inc.

Contents

ABOUT THE AUTHORS   vii

NOTE TO THE READER   ix

FOREWORD   xi

1. WHAT IS DELEGATION?   1

Introduction – definitions: delegation, responsibility, authority, accountability – assignment by function – coordination and uniformity of activity – investing authority – how delegating benefits the manager and the corporation – responsibility – authority – accountability – summary and quiz.

2. WHEN DO YOU DELEGATE?   21

Introduction – handling a "hot potato" – feedback – appraising subordinates – delegating detailed work – jobs that require a manager's status – rewards and punishments – developing subordinates' skills – testing subordinates – summary and quiz.

3. HOW DO YOU DELEGATE?   40

Introduction – setting objectives and making them understood – written assignments – assigning responsibility and setting target dates – establishing controls – communication systems – summary and quiz.

4. TO WHOM DO YOU DELEGATE?   69

Introduction – observing levels of command – equalizing the work load – developing subordinates – specialization – levels of capability – avoiding the obvious – testing ability – summary and quiz.

5. PROBLEMS OF DELEGATION 96

Introduction – the reluctance to delegate and the reluctance to accept delegation – fear of ignorance – detail and the level of command – the do-it-yourself compulsion – fear of competition – letting a subordinate learn from mistakes – definition of objectives – taking the easy way out – overdependence – fear of criticism – lack of confidence – individual identification with company goals – quiz and summary.

INDEX 123

ABOUT THE AUTHORS

NEELY D. GARDNER is eminently qualified to prepare material in the field of management development. For many years he was director of training for the California State Personnel Board. In that capacity he helped develop and implement the methods and procedures which have given that state's civil servants such an excellent performance record.

In 1962, he was named deputy director (administration) for the California Water Resources Agency.

Mr. Gardner has served as a consultant to the United Nations in establishing personnel training for governments of underdeveloped countries. In addition, he is a frequent consultant on training problems for major industrial firms in the West.

* * *

JOHN N. DAVIS, who served as advisory editor for this program, is Assistant Professor of Management and Industrial Relations at the School of Commerce, Accounts, and Finance of New York University.

In his work as an educator and as a consultant to business and industry in the field of management development, Professor Davis calls upon a unique blend of experience (he is a retired United States Army Colonel) and education (United States Military Academy at West Point and Ohio State University).

NOTE TO THE READER

This is not an ordinary book. Although its pages are numbered in the usual way, they are not always read in the usual order. The material is divided into convenient sections, and at the end of each section you will find instructions indicating which section is to be read next. Please follow the instructions carefully.

You will find that reading this book is very much like having an individual tutor. The book will continually ask you questions and correct your errors while it gives you information.

Your progress through this course will depend wholly on your ability to choose right answers. We recommend that you not try to go through the whole course in one sitting, or even two or three. As a rule, several short learning sessions are more productive than one or two long ones.

Follow instructions accurately and you will find it difficult to reach the final section without obtaining a good grasp of the fundamentals of delegating.

FOREWORD

Survival in today's highly intricate world of business—a world complicated by new and dynamic methods of production, transportation, marketing, and communications—depends upon the successful utilization of employee ability. The manager cannot "do it all" himself. If he is to be a successful manager, he must get his work done through others. He must define organizational objectives, ensure that they are understood, and fix responsibility for their achievement; in short, he must *delegate*.

Effective delegation of responsibility and authority to others will help achieve the production or service goals of an organization; inept of minimal delegation will hinder such achievement. In the last analysis, *delegation is the measure of a manager*.

A dominant question in any discussion of management improvement is this: "How can we bring about greater and more effective delegation?" Recognition of the benefits of delegation is universal, but there is a sizable gap between *knowing* that delegation is necessary and *achieving* it successfully. The purpose of this course is to close that gap—to help managers realize the value of delegation, understand what and how to delegate, and know how to overcome the forces working against delegation.

This TutorText® course uses the method of programed instruction developed by Norman A. Crowder, Vice President and Technical Director of the Educational Science Division of U. S. Industries, Inc. Ed Orloff, Editorial Director of the Educational Science Division, encouraged the development of this and other TutorText volumes—*Effective Executive Practices* and *Better Business Organization*.

Special acknowledgement should be made of the influence of Dr. Frank Sherwood of the University of Southern California and Dr.

Joseph Trickett of the University of Santa Clara. Great help also came from the many practicing executives from business and government who took this course in its testing phase and helped to clarify, modify, and strengthen the material.

NEELY D. GARDNER
Sacramento, California

JOHN N. DAVIS
New York, N.Y.

THE ART OF DELEGATING

Chapter 1

WHAT IS DELEGATION?

Many management experts believe that delegation of work is the most essential function of the manager. The effectiveness of his delegation is a measure of his managerial talent.

Here are some things to consider about the nature of delegation:

1. As an enterprise or organization grows, it is impossible for a manager to perform all the necessary jobs himself. He must call upon others for assistance.

2. Delegating managerial responsibilities to more than one employee requires managers and employees to coordinate their activities.

3. A manager delegates work (jobs) to others in order to extend himself. To be effective as a manager, he must accomplish work through others.

4. A manager should not delegate all of the jobs that he has to do.

5. A manager delegates *authority* to others to act for him.

6. Delegation of authority should be accompanied by delegation of *responsibility* and *accountability*.

7. Cooperative effort has made modern industrial organization succeed. Delegation is necessary to provide more complete services and higher productivity.

To help you understand the course material that follows, we are going to define the terms *delegation, responsibility, authority,* and *accountability.* You should know and understand each of them.

DELEGATION: Giving others the authority to act in your behalf, accompanying it with responsibility and accountability for
results.

RESPONSIBILITY: The job you and your organization are
given to do—as one company phrases it, "the duties of a
position."

AUTHORITY: The right to make decisions, take action, and
give orders.

ACCOUNTABILITY: Your liability to your superior and your
obligation to accept responsibilities and use authority.

Now we would like to use a very simple example to illustrate
some principles and practices of delegation.

Sam Green started a small store, the Green Front Grocery, in a
new neighborhood. As the neighborhood grew, business grew, until
it got to be more than Sam could handle by himself. Soon he had to
hire more help. Sam was then faced with a decision about how to
divide the work (jobs). This could be done in several ways. Which of
the following would you say is the better way?

Turn to the section that corresponds to the answer you choose.

Assign definite parts of the store to his employees. **section 8**

Assign the new men to certain jobs, such as sweeping the store, replacing stock, and checking out groceries at the cash register. **section 20**

2

You are here by mistake, for you could not have reached this section by following directions. We repeat: This book is not put together like ordinary books.

The material has been divided into convenient sections. At the end of each section of information there is a question, and the answer you choose from among the choices given will indicate the specific section you are to turn to next. If your answer is wrong, you are asked to go back and try again. If your answer is right, you move on to new material.

We think you should go back now to the section above and begin again, this time following the directions.

[from section 19]

YOUR ANSWER: Your power and right to make decisions, to take action, and to give orders is called *accountability*.

This is not correct.

In the delegation process the manager gives others the right to act in his behalf. They then have the authority to make choices, to do what is necessary to get the job done, and to ask others to take necessary action. They have an obligation to act in behalf of the boss, to assume the necessary duties, and to execute the task. In others words, they are accountable; accountability is the subordinate's obligation to carry out responsibility and to use authority.

Right now we are trying to help you remember some of the definitions we have given of such terms as delegation, responsibility, authority, and accountability. If you will keep this purpose in mind it may help you choose the correct response.

If you think you are now on the right track, please go back to section 19 and make another choice.

4

[from section 12]

YOUR ANSWER: Sam was assigning work to others while retaining the authority and accountability for the work.

This is not correct.

Sam assigned areas of responsibility to his men and asked the manager to run the store for him. This action sounds to us as if it meets our definition of delegation: Giving others the authority to act in one's behalf, accompanying it with responsibility and accountability for results.

Please return to section 12 and make another choice.

5

[from section 31]

YOUR ANSWER: Authority means giving the power or right to make decisions, to take action, and to give orders.

You are correct.

When we assign authority, we give the subordinate the right to take action and make decisions which are required to get the job done. Then we hold him answerable for proper use of authority and for carrying out the duties of the position. We are holding him accountable for results. We do not tell him how to do the job. Authority and responsibility are not separated.

Having dealt with the definitions of *delegation, responsibility,* and *authority,* we are now ready to look at an illustration which should give us a better understanding of *accountability.*

At a meeting with his five store managers, Sam said, "You all say you have a good idea of the duties of your position and that you understand your authority. Now I'm going to hold you accountable for the operation of your stores."

What is the best definition of accountability?

Accountability is a system for reporting the action that has been taken as a result of delegation. **section 14**

Accountability is the follow-up process instituted to assure execution of the delegated task. **section 25**

Accountability means the subordinate's obligation to carry out responsibilities and use authority. **section 33**

6

[from section 23]

YOUR ANSWER: Delegation is important in an industrial society
because it permits managers to create bigger businesses by extending themselves.

This is not correct.

Our society constantly moves to improve the standard of living
of individuals; and business, as part of that society, constantly tries
to expand. But this is not exactly what we had in mind. Delegation
makes it possible to improve the standard of living because it multi-
plies ability.

Please return to section 23 and make another choice.

7

[from section 33]

YOUR ANSWER: The job you and your organization are given to
do as you administer the affairs of others is called your *obligation*.

This is not the correct answer. Obligation is the acceptance of
responsibility.

We are talking about the things that constitute the duties of your
position. At the moment we are checking with you to see if you
remember the definitions we gave you for:

Delegation
Responsibility
Authority
Accountability

Return to section 33 and make another choice.

8

[from section 1]

YOUR ANSWER: To divide the work, Sam could assign definite parts of the store to his employees.

No, this is not the best advice.

It is possible to divide work on a geographic or location basis. But in the case of a small store, it is not practical to divide the work this way. It is better if work is assigned according to function, such as taking telephone orders, stocking shelves, checking out groceries at the check stand, and so on. Turn back to section 1 and select the other answer.

9

[from section 16]

YOUR ANSWER: Responsibility means transferring the responsibility or a segment of the work from yourself to a subordinate.

This is not correct.

Assigning responsibility does not relieve you of that same responsibility. When sales drop off in the meat department, Mark Rathbone holds the meat manager responsible. Mark in turn is held responsible by Sam. Both the subordinate and the superior are responsible for the results, good and bad.

Go back to section 16 and make another choice.

10

[from section 21]

YOUR ANSWER: The obligation of a subordinate to accept responsibilities and use authority is called *accountability*.

You are correct.

Delegation is investing in others the authority to act in your behalf; accountability is one portion of delegation. Accountability is a type of obligation.

We have spent a good deal of time on definitions. We have done so because having the terms defined will be of great assistance to you as you proceed with the study of delegation. Let us summarize:

Delegation: Giving others the authority to act in your behalf, accompanying it with responsibility and accountability for results.

Responsibility: The job you and your organization are given to do—as one organization phrases it, "the duties of a position."

Authority: The right to make decisions, take action, and give orders.

Accountability: Your liability to answer to your superior and your obligation to accept responsibilities and use authority.

In addition to answering the question "What is delegation?" we explained why we delegate. In this section we have said:

A manager usually accomplishes work through others; he delegates to extend himself.

Teamwork or mutual effort is not possible unless responsibilities are shared. A manager delegates so that more than one person can contribute toward a common goal.

Delegation is necessary to provide more complete services and higher productivity.

Delegation of a manager's responsibilities to more than one employee requires that managers and employees coordinate their activities.

We are now ready to see how much you have learned in this section. Go on to the next section for a test question.

11
[from section 10]

TEST QUESTION

Select the answer that best completes the following sentence: We delegate because . . .

selection is difficult, many workmen are highly skilled, communications are improving, and delegation lessens fear of criticism. **section 18** it permits the manager to extend himself, utilizes individual abilities, makes teamwork possible, and increases productivity. **section 24**

delegation puts the burden where it belongs, makes the manager aware of minute details, and tests the competence of employees. **section 29**

it improves the manager's sense of security, is comfortable to dependent persons, avoids conflict situations, makes communications easier, and does not increase individual workload. **section 34**

12

[*from section 20*]

YOUR ANSWER: Coordination was the greater need.

Right. As the business expanded, Sam had to assign tasks (extend himself) and get his work done by delegation. But then he had to work at pulling together the efforts of these individuals. The more stores he opened, the greater was the need for this coordination.

When an executive delegates he gives employees tasks and duties to perform. He also holds them liable for designated performance. Most important, he vests the employee with the right to carry out the assigned duty just as if the executive were doing the job himself. When the Green Front Grocery expanded to a multiple store operation, Sam had to hire additional men to run the new stores. He assigned personnel in each store as follows: a vegetable counter man, a man to head the meat department, and a man to head the general grocery department. All of these were overseen by a manager. Sam told the manager, "I want you to run this business as it should be run, and you will be given credit for the store's success or failures."

In effect, what was Sam doing?

Assigning work to others while retaining the authority and accountability for the work. **section 4**

Investing with authority to act in his behalf. **section 23**

Requiring subordinates to do assigned work in a manner and by a method satisfactory to himself. **section 32**

YOUR ANSWER: Your power and right to make decisions, to take action, and to give orders is called *administration*.

This is not correct.

Utilization of your power and right to make decisions, take action, and give orders is certainly a part of the administrative process, just as are all other management functions.

But right now we are trying to help you remember our definitions of delegation, responsibility, authority, and accountability. If you will keep this purpose in mind it may help you choose the correct responses.

If you think you are now on the right track, go back to section 19 and make another choice.

YOUR ANSWER: Accountability is a system for reporting the action that has been taken as a result of delegation.

Reporting is generally considered to be a part of a management control system. It is a very necessary function in large organizations. But "a system for reporting" is not accountability.

When a person is made accountable for carrying out an action, he has an obligation to do the assigned work by making decisions, taking action, and using authority.

There is a better answer. Please return to section 5 and make another choice.

YOUR ANSWER: When you authorize others to act in your behalf, it is called *vacillation*.

This is not correct.

Vacillation occurs when a person is unable to make up his mind or arrive at a decision, leaning first one way, then another.

We are talking about the process of extending yourself so that you can get work done through others. Doesn't this sound familiar now? What we are talking about is the topic of this whole lesson.

Please go back to section 27 and make another choice.

16

[from section 23]

YOUR ANSWER: Delegation is important in an industrial society because it permits managers to extend themselves, thus increasing products and services.

You are correct.

Effective delegation makes it possible to multiply ability by getting work done through others.

Our industrial society could not exist unless the manager were able to get his work done through others. Certainly one manager could not, through his efforts alone, manufacture all the goods that are produced or render all the services that are provided. He must achieve the purposes of the enterprise by seeing that people work together.

To achieve success, the manager always retains responsibility for the job to be done; but he also shares this responsibility with his subordinate.

Now let us deal with another facet of delegation.

Mark Rathbone, manager of Green Front Store No. 2, told his meat department manager: "You are completely responsible for the meat. I don't want to have to worry about your department, and I don't intend to."

Within two or three months, meat sales dropped considerably. When Sam talked to Mark about the drop-off in meat sales, Mark said, "It's not my fault. I turned meat over to Sid. It's his responsibility."

Below are three descriptions of responsibility. Which of the definitions is applicable to this situation?

Responsibility means transferring the responsibility for a segment of the work from yourself to a subordinate. **section 9**

10

Responsibility means the accountability you have for seeing that the job gets done. You can make subordinates solely responsible for activities carried on by the segment of the organization for which you are responsible. **section 22**

Responsibility means delegating the proper amount of authority and responsibility for the job you and your organization are given to do. Therefore, both you and your subordinate are responsible. **section 31**

17
[from section 31]

YOUR ANSWER: Authority means giving notice that decision-making has been delegated to a particular individual.

This is not the expected answer.

Giving a person authority is more than a paper assignment. It is giving him the actual power to execute the task which has been assigned. Authority comes to the individual not only because he is given control of certain amounts of money, the right to utilize materials for specified reasons, and the right to utilize the skills and knowledge of certain employees to further the well-being of the enterprise.

There is a better answer. Please go back to section 31 and make another choice.

18
[from section 11]

YOUR TEST ANSWER: We delegate because selection is difficult, many workmen are highly skilled, communications are improving, and delegation lessens fear of criticism.

We think your choice is incorrect. We agree that selection is difficult. We agree that many workmen are highly skilled. We hope that communications are improving.

But none of these answers the question "Why do we delegate?"

Furthermore, delegation heightens the fear of criticism, rather than lessening it. One of the reasons some people do not delegate

11

is because they are afraid they will be blamed for the presumed inadequacies of those to whom they may assign jobs.

Go back to section 11 and choose a better answer.

19

[from section 33]

YOUR ANSWER: The job you and your organization are given to do as you administer the affairs of others is called your *responsibility*.

You are correct.

The responsibilities of an individual are the *duties of his position*. This differs from accountability, with which it is sometimes confused, in that accountability is the individual's liability to answer to superiors and his obligation to accept responsibilities and use authority.

Now let us go on to another definition.

Your power and right to make decisions, to take action, and to give orders is called:

Accountability. **section 3**

Administration. **section 13**

Authority. **section 27**

20

[from section 1]

YOUR ANSWER: To divide the work, Sam could assign the new men to certain jobs, such as sweeping the store, replacing stock, and checking out groceries at the cash register.

You are correct. It is possible to divide work on a location basis, but this isn't practical in a small store, where assignment by function makes better sense; as Sam expanded, he assigned certain tasks to the two clerks he had hired.

Time passed and Sam's business continued to prosper. He expanded to *five* Green Front Grocery stores located in two different communities. He soon found himself spending a great deal of time in travel between stores. He realized that he could not leave the stores to run themselves; each store needed a boss. But even after the bosses were appointed the stores differed considerably.

Sam found that one of his tasks was getting all the stores to work toward the same ends. He also found that he had to give others the job of acting in his behalf; in other words, he had to delegate authority.

In the Green Front Grocery chain, what would you say was the greater need at this stage?

Coordination. **section 12**

Uniformity of action. **section 30**

21
[from section 27]

YOUR ANSWER: When you authorize others to act in your behalf it is called *delegation*.

You are correct.

Delegation means that you give others the power to act for you and that you require them to answer to you. Delegation is one portion of the administrative process, not the whole package. But delegation is the measure of a manager, because only insofar as he delegates can he extend himself and get work done through others.

Let us see what you can do with the next definition.

The obligation of a subordinate to accept responsibilities and use authority is called:

Accountability. **section 10**

Acceptability. **section 28**

22
[from section 16]

YOUR ANSWER: Responsibility means the accountability you have for seeing that the job gets done. You can make subordinates solely responsible for activities carried on by the segment of the organization for which you are responsible.

No.

The person to whom you delegate should be held accountable for

13

the success of the task. In other words, he has responsibility for effective execution of the job delegated to him. But there is one aspect of responsibility not covered in your answer. Even when you have delegated, *you* are still accountable for the success or failure of the job undertaken. You cannot divest yourself of responsibility for the job delegated.

This is one of the most trying facets of delegation. Because the manager must retain responsibility as well as delegate responsibility, there is a risk involved if the subordinate does not carry out the task in an effective manner.

Go back to section 16 and make another choice.

23
[from section 12]

YOUR ANSWER: Sam was investing others with authority to act in his behalf.

Correct.

We have defined delegation as giving others the authority to act in one's behalf, accompanying it with responsibility and accountability for results. Sam retains responsibility for the operation of the stores, but he is also delegating responsibility to the managers.

Remember, delegation is the means by which the productivity of the manager is increased.

Let's evaluate Sam's experience. Why do you think delegation is of such importance in an industrial society?

It permits managers to create bigger businesses by extending themselves. **section 6**

It permits managers to extend themselves, thus increasing products and services. **section 16**

24
[from section 11]

[from section 11]

YOUR TEST ANSWER: We delegate because delegation permits the manager to extend himself, utilizes individual abilities, makes teamwork possible, and increases productivity.

14

You are correct.

We have seen, in the case of the Green Front Grocery chain, that Sam was able to increase services to his community by hiring more people and delegating tasks for them to perform.

Without this additional help and without the delegation, the communities would have had to look elsewhere for services or do without them.

Delegation makes teamwork possible. And it certainly increases productivity, for there are many things that cannot be accomplished by the individual but must be accomplished through group effort.

You have answered this test question successfully. Please go on now to section 36 and Chapter 2.

25
[from section 5]

YOUR ANSWER: Accountability is the follow-up process instituted to assure execution of the delegated task.

Follow-up or inspection is certainly a necessary step in the management control process, but this does not define the term accountability.

When a person is accountable for the execution of a job or task, he has the obligation to make decisions, take action, assume responsibility, and use the authority that has been given to him.

There is a better answer. Please go back to section 5 and make another choice.

26
[from section 33]

YOUR ANSWER: The job you and your organization are given to do as you administer the affairs of others is called your *accountability*.

This is not the expected answer.

Accountability is the liability a person has to answer to his superior and the obligation to accept assignments and use authority.

Please go back to section 33 and make another choice.

27

[from section 19]

YOUR ANSWER: Your power and right to make decisions, to take action, and to give orders is called *authority*.

You are correct.

Authority is the key to the managerial job. Authority comes from the relative position of the job in the organization. The higher the position the more the authority, and vice versa. Authority is a component of administration, but administration encompasses a great deal more than authority.

Having defined authority, let us go on to another definition.

When you authorize others to act in your behalf, it is called:

Vacillation. **section 15**

Delegation. **section 21**

Administration. **section 35**

28

[from section 21]

YOUR ANSWER: The obligation of a subordinate to accept responsibilities and use authority is called *acceptability*.

No, this is not the correct definition.

Acceptability is not a term used in the field of management. It has not been used in any part of this lesson.

Please go back to section 21 and choose the other answer.

29

[from section 11]

YOUR TEST ANSWER: We delegate because delegation puts the burden where it belongs, makes the manager aware of minute details, and tests the competence of employees.

This is not correct.

Let us analyze the statements one by one.

Delegation puts the burden where it belongs. Frequently it does. However, it is not the purpose of delegation to place the burden upon anybody, but to get the work done through other people. Once again we should remember that *the manager remains responsible.* He does not rid himself of the burden.

Delegation makes the manager aware of minute details. Quite the contrary. He does not concern himself with minute details when he has delegated.

Delegation tests the competence of employees. This is true to a great degree, and it happens to be one of the very important uses of delegation. Nevertheless, the total paragraph did not answer the question "Why do we delegate?"

Go back to section 11 and choose a better answer.

30
[*from section 20*]

YOUR ANSWER: Uniformity of action was the greater need.

This is not so.

When an organization has activities in a number of locations, or a number of people carrying on like activities in one location, coordination of these activities is a must. The greater the number, the greater the need for someone to act as a coordinator of all of the efforts.

Please go back to section 20 and choose the other answer.

31
[*from section 16*]

YOUR ANSWER: Responsibility means delegating the proper amount of authority and responsibility for the job you and your organization are given to do. Therefore, both you and your subordinate are responsible.

You are correct.

The person to whom you delegate is held accountable for effective execution of the task; he is responsible. Likewise, *you* are responsible for the success or failure of the job undertaken.

YOU CANNOT DIVEST YOURSELF OF THE RESPONSI-
BILITY.

Remember, delegation means giving authority to others to act in
one's behalf, with commensurate responsibility and accountability
for results.

Responsibility is the job the manager and his organization are
given to do, or as one organization has defined it, "the duties of a
position."

Now for the meaning of *authority*.

Over at Green Front Grocery No. 4, Manager Wilbur Potts tells
Attlee Baer: "You are responsible for the vegetable department.
You report on sales and condition of produce, and take inventory.
Then I'll tell you what you can do and how you can do it. I'll make
the decisions for you."

When Sam heard about this he said, "I guess I'd better explain
what is meant by 'authority' when we talk about 'delegating responsibility and authority.'"

If you were in Sam's place, what would your definition of authority be?

Giving the power or right to make decisions, to take action, and to
give orders. **section 5**

Giving notice that decision-making has been delegated to a particular
individual. **section 17**

32

[*from section 12*]

YOUR ANSWER: Sam was requiring subordinates to do assigned
work in a manner and by a method satisfactory to himself.

Perhaps, but we have no evidence that this is so.

As we understand the assignment, it was a rather broad one,
with the store manager being responsible for running the business.
At this point we do not think that Sam was giving detailed instructions for day-to-day operation.

Our definition of delegation: Giving others the authority to act
in one's behalf, accompanying it with responsibility and accountability for results.

It appears to us that Sam was conveying such authority in this particular instance.

Please go back to section 12 and make another choice.

YOUR ANSWER: Accountability means the subordinate's obligation to carry out responsibilities and use authority.

You are correct.

A subordinate has a liability to answer to his superior. He is obligated to accept responsibility for making decisions, taking action, and using authority that has been vested in him in order to assure the proper execution of his position. This is accountability.

Reporting and follow-up systems are important parts of management controls, but they are not a part of accountability. They merely indicate whether the delegated tasks—the ones for which the employee will be held accountable—are being executed.

We have covered our definitions of delegation, responsibility, authority, and accountability in an illustrative fashion. Now we would like to spend a little time in checking to see if you recognize such definitions.

For example, the job you and your organization are given to do as you administer the affairs of others is called your:

Obligation. **section 7**

Responsibility. **section 19**

Accountability. **section 26**

YOUR TEST ANSWER: We delegate because it improves the manager's sense of security, is comfortable to dependent persons, avoids conflict situations, makes communications easier, and does not increase individual workload.

Nothing could be further from the truth.

The reason many people do not delegate is because delegation taxes their sense of security to a great extent. After all, others are carrying out tasks assigned by the manager, and he cannot be completely certain how well they will do. Delegation makes dependent persons very uncomfortable because they cannot take the strain of responsibility.

Delegation does not avoid conflict situations, although it does not necessarily increase them. Delegation places a burden upon the manager to communicate well; and delegation frequently increases the individual workload of persons under the manager, although not necessarily so.

Go back to section 11 and choose a better answer.

35
[from section 27]

YOUR ANSWER: When you authorize others to act in your behalf it is called *administration*.

This is not correct.

Administration encompasses many things: delegation, planning, organization, controlling, and other important management functions.

In this definition we are talking about the very heart of the lesson you are undertaking. We are talking about the process of assigning tasks to others in order that we can extend ourselves. We are talking about getting work done through others. Now this sounds familiar, does it not? Please return to section 27 and make another choice.

Chapter 2

WHEN DO YOU DELEGATE?

One of your duties as a manager is to determine those things which only you should do and which are, therefore, not usually delegated. For example, you *should:*

a. Handle your own "hot potatoes."

Emergency situations requiring *your* skill and knowledge.

Extremely important matters that have serious consequences.

Matters of exception to general policy and routine procedure.

b. Conduct appraisals of your subordinates.

c. Reward or punish subordinates (levy sanctions).

d. Do the jobs requiring your status and position.

You also determine those things you need not do yourself and therefore usually delegate:

a. Routine and inconsequential details.

To your secretary

To staff assistants

b. Tasks and duties that others can handle as well or better than yourself—jobs which use specialized skills of subordinates.

c. Activities that will lead to the development of subordinates and test their abilities.

When do you delegate and when do you handle your own "hot potatoes"? Let's examine that question by taking a look at what happened to Sam when he was faced with the same problem.

Sam's Green Front Grocery chain prospered. George Gable was doing a good job of managing Store No. 1. However, the produce man, Jay Kern, was rather inexperienced and on one occasion over-bought on bananas. This mistake could have caused a serious monetary loss, unless other stores in the chain helped by taking and selling some of the excess bananas.

In these circumstances, George Gable should:

21

Delegate to Jay Kern the job of telling Sam of the problem and negotiating with other stores to take surplus bananas. **section 44**

Take on himself the job of informing Sam of the problem and negotiating with other store managers to absorb the excess bananas.

section 52

37

[from section 42]

YOUR ANSWER: You should delegate the promotion of immediate subordinates.

This is not correct.

One of the tasks which you certainly should *not* delegate is the promotion of your immediate subordinates. These subordinates report to you; they are persons with whom you should work carefully. It is also generally true that a person should be hired or fired by his immediate superior. There are of course exceptions to this, but in general we can accept this as being true.

There is a better answer. Please go back to section 42 and make another choice.

38

[from section 66]

YOUR ANSWER: Development of employees will not be accomplished by delegating special projects and assignments that will test the employees' abilities.

This is not correct.

One useful contribution that effective delegation can make to an organization is the testing of the skills and abilities of subordinates. One way to test such skills and abilities is by the assignment of special projects. It is generally accepted that delegation is an excellent way to bring about the development of employees. In this question we are talking about exceptions to this statement.

There is a better answer. Please return to section 66 and make another choice.

YOUR ANSWER: The best advice to a manager is this: Let the personnel officer appraise your subordinates.

This is not the correct answer.

One of the things which a manager must not delegate is the appraisal of his subordinate's performance. In order to delegate, a manager must know the capabilities of those who work immediately under him. Not only must he appraise them in order to know what kinds of jobs they can undertake, but he needs to appraise them in order to know the developmental activity in which they should engage.

We think there is a much better answer. Please go back to section 51 and make another choice.

YOUR ANSWER: Mark should fire the clerk himself.

You are correct.

The manager should not delegate to staff assistants or other personnel the job of levying sanctions or giving rewards. The person who hires and fires—the person who levies sanctions and gives rewards—assumes a position of influence that could detract from the influence of the manager.

So far we have said that the manager should *not* delegate the hot potatoes, the appraisal of subordinates, the job of giving rewards and punishments, or the jobs requiring the executive's own status and position.

The manager *should* delegate jobs that are routine and inconsequential; tasks and duties that others can handle as well as or better than the manager himself; activities that will lead to the development of subordinates and test their abilities.

When Wilbur Potts, manager of Green Front Grocery No. 4, went on vacation, he called in Attlee Baer and said, "I'm leaving you in full charge of the store while I am away. You have the same authority I have to make decisions, take action, and give orders. Good luck!"

With which of the following statements do you agree?

In putting Attlee Baer in charge of the store during his absence, Potts was able to turn over to Baer complete responsibility for operating the store. **section 48**

In putting Attlee Baer in charge of the store during his absence, Potts delegated activities which were likely to help Baer develop as a manager.

section 58

41

[from section 64]

YOUR ANSWER: The secretary's suggestion was a good one. In checking the daily totals, Sam was doing detailed work that he should have delegated.

You are correct.

Sam should delegate to others the things that they can do and keep for himself the things that only he can do.

In general, a manager should devote his time to the functions of long-range planning and organization, which require his personal presence and skill. As the owner of the Green Front Groceries, Sam has a certain prestige and authority which he should not attempt to delegate.

Despite occasional setbacks in Sam's attempts to become a full-fledged manager, he had been building his business quite well and had, in fact, established himself as a successful businessman. But, as in all expanding businesses, there came a time when the Green Front Groceries needed financial assistance. Store No. 1 was outmoded and needed to be modernized in keeping with the four newer stores in the chain. Sam, therefore, needed money for the renovation. Although the new controller was familiar with all the details of the financial situation, Sam decided that he himself must take responsibility for arranging to borrow the money; he felt that the controller simply did not have the prestige, status, and position to negotiate with the bank for the loan of money.

What do you think?

Sam probably had a good point in deciding to negotiate personally with the banker, rather than delegating this task to his controller.

section 53

Sam probably was mistaken in not sending his controller to negotiate with the banker for the building loan. **section 62**

42

[from section 51]

YOUR ANSWER: The best advice to a manager is this: Handle your own hot potatoes.

Correct.

The manager is responsible for the mistakes of his subordinates. Under certain conditions—if the mistakes are bad enough or if conditions have deteriorated enough or if the risk is of a crucial nature —the manager himself should step in and attempt to handle the problem. This is particularly true if the activity involves outside organizations or superiors.

Test Question No. 2.

Which of the jobs listed below should you delegate?

The promotion of immediate subordinates. **section 37**

The decision to negotiate a loan. **section 54**

The tasks and duties that others can handle as well as you. **section 66**

43

[from section 58]

YOUR ANSWER: In letting Rocky Richards try out as a checker during a slow time of day, the store manager was delegating a job that probably should be reserved for a more experienced person.

This is not the answer we hoped you would give.

It is true that checkers are usually more mature persons, and that a box boy must have some seasoning before he can take full responsibility as a checker at a cash register. Nevertheless, it appears as if Potts were beginning to teach Rocky Richards some new skills and to see how much added responsibility he could handle. The trial experience occurred during a slow time of day when errors would tend to show up more quickly, and Rocky Richards would not be hard pressed at the check stand.

We think there is a better answer. Please return to section 58 and make another choice.

44

[from section 36]

YOUR ANSWER: George Gable should delegate to Jay Kern the job of telling Sam of the problem and negotiating with other stores to take surplus bananas.

This is not correct.

Certainly Jay Kern should be faced with his mistake and should feel responsible for assisting in any way possible in recouping the loss. Nevertheless, this situation represents a hot potato that George Gable should himself handle with the boss. It might be that George should do most of the negotiating with other store managers, although it is possible that Jay Kern could be helpful here.

Please go back to section 36 and choose the other answer.

45

[from section 52]

YOUR ANSWER: Send the personnel director to all stores. A trained personnel man knows people and can detect inefficiency. This will relieve Sam of some of the work.

This is not correct.

A trained personnel man can spot weaknesses which might escape other eyes, and he can recommend corrective action, but having him do the job is a sure road to trouble. Personnel appraisal is a job that a manager cannot successfully delegate.

In order to find out how his subordinates are performing, a manager must look and see for himself. A personnel director will not judge employees through the manager's eyes. In addition, a certain amount of resentment could develop from having a "third party" spy out inefficient work.

Please go back to section 52 and choose another answer.

46
[from section 65]

YOUR ANSWER: Mark should have the personnel director fire the clerk.

This is not the expected answer.

Managers should not delegate their functions to staff personnel. If the personnel director is the person who hires and fires people, he begins to assume power and influence and authority that belongs to the manager.

In our opinion, the personnel director should neither levy sanctions nor give rewards. These are the jobs of the manager himself.

We think there is a better answer. Please go back to section 65 and make another choice.

47
[from section 53]

YOUR ANSWER: Seeing Sam working the early morning produce market, I would say, "I am glad Sam's still able to get out and be one of the boys. It boosts morale."

This would not be a wise reaction.

One of the myths against which we operate is the belief that the manager must be able to do it better to boot.

If a manager is to extend himself, he obviously cannot personally engage in the great number and wide variety of activities performed by those under him. Neither should he expect to have greater proficiency than each subordinate in each of the tasks. Let's face it; Sam made his way to produce row early every morning to engage in the bargaining, bartering, and buying because he liked to do so, not because it was good management to do so. There is a better answer.

Please go back to section 53 and make another choice.

48

[from section 40]

YOUR ANSWER: In putting Attlee Baer in charge of the store during his absence, Potts was able to turn over to Baer complete responsibility for operating the store.

This is not correct.

Potts cannot get out from under his responsibility. If something were to go wrong during his absence, he would suffer just as much as the man left in charge of the store. Actually, Potts is giving Baer an opportunity to run the store with full authority to make decisions, take action, and give orders. With this experience, and if he has "what it takes," Baer should be a better employee and more competent to eventually become a manager.

There is a better answer. Please go back to section 40 and make another choice.

49

[from section 66]

YOUR ANSWER: Development of employees will not be accomplished by delegating duties that can be assigned and handled on a temporary basis.

This is not correct.

Our assumption is that an excellent way to bring about the development of employees is through the process of delegation. As they assume greater responsibility, they learn more skills and develop their abilities to a higher degree. One of the ways that delegation can assist in enlarging the scope of employee activities is through temporary assignments and duties.

In this question we are talking about certain things that cannot or should not be delegated for the purpose of developing employees. Often, temporary duties *should* be delegated. We believe that in this case you are mistaken. Please go back to section 66 and make another choice.

YOUR ANSWER: In letting Rocky Richards try out as a checker during a slow time of day, the store manager was probably testing Rocky's ability to handle greater responsibility.

You are correct.

Potts chose a propitious time of day to let Rocky try his hand at running the cash register and checking out groceries. It was a time when the consequences could not be serious, yet it was a time that could partially test Rocky's ability to handle greater responsibility in the store.

One of the answers to the question "When do you delegate?" is: *You sometimes delegate when the projects, tasks, and activities that you assign will test the abilities of the subordinates to whom you delegate.*

Now let us summarize what we have studied in this lesson.

YOU DELEGATE THINGS YOU NEED NOT DO YOUR-SELF.

Determine which things you should not delegate. For example, you alone should:

a. Handle your own "hot potatoes."
b. Appraise your immediate subordinates.
c. Reward and punish subordinates.
d. Do jobs requiring your status and position.

Determine which things you should delegate. For example, you delegate:

a. Routine and inconsequential details; use your secretary, staff, and other assistants.
b. Tasks and duties that others can handle as well or better; use specialized skills of subordinates.
c. Activities that will lead to the development of subordinates and that will test abilities.

You are now ready to test your knowledge of the material in this section. Please proceed to the Test Sequence starting with the next section.

51

[from section 50]

TEST

Question No. 1.

Based on the preceding decision of delegation, which one of the following precepts provides the best advice to a manager?

Let the personnel officer appraise your subordinates. **section 39**

Handle your own hot potatoes. **section 42**

Call on your technical staff to reward and punish employees, once such action seems necessary. **section 57**

Never delegate for the purpose of training. **section 63**

52

[from section 36]

YOUR ANSWER: George Gable should take on himself the job of informing Sam of the problem and negotiating with other store managers to absorb the excess bananas.

This is correct.

This situation is definitely a hot potato. A serious loss will result unless the mistake is rectified. It is the store manager's job to inform Sam of a mistake of this nature and magnitude. This does not mean that Jay Kern should not feel responsible and be held accountable for the error; he must be made aware of the seriousness of the problem so that he will not make such errors in the future.

The manager should not delegate the hot potatoes. But on the other hand, employees must be made aware of how they are doing. It is the supervisor's job to assess the work of his subordinates.

At headquarters of the Green Front Grocery chain, Sam was kept very busy, particularly in matters of finance and personnel. Sam's work increased so much that he had to hire two assistants, a personnel director and a controller. Shortly after having hired these two assistants, Sam decided to check on the effectiveness of all his store managers.

What is the best procedure for doing this?

Send the personnel director to all stores. A trained personnel man knows people and can detect inefficiency. This will relieve Sam of some of the work. **section 45**

Send both the personnel director and the controller. Using two experts will give Sam more information sooner. **section 59**

Sam should go himself in order to get firsthand knowledge of how the managers are doing and make corrections on the spot. **section 64**

53

[from section 41]

YOUR ANSWER: Sam probably had a good point in deciding to negotiate personally with the banker, rather than delegating this task to his controller.

You are correct.

Sam did not delegate the job to his controller. Sam knew that his status as a successful businessman would be of value in negotiating the loan. Furthermore, Sam felt that the banker might resent having to deal with the controller. Under these circumstances, Sam decided he could do better than the controller. His point was well taken. *The manager should not delegate those things which require his status* to assure their effective execution.

We have discussed Sam's insistence upon personally running the day's total on the adding machine. Sam also could not get over his love for the produce market where he had purchased wholesale fruits and vegetables when he was a one-man store owner. Many an early morning saw him down on produce row working shoulder to shoulder with his buyers. If you were asked whether such an activity were proper for the president of a grocery store chain, what would you say?

"I am glad to see Sam is still able to get out and be one of the boys. It boosts morale." **section 47**

"There are people in the organization who can do the buying job as well as or better than Sam. Why doesn't he let them do it?" **section 65**

54

[from section 42]

YOUR ANSWER: You should delegate the decision to negotiate a loan.

This is not correct.

In general, the manager does not delegate to his subordinate those jobs that require the prestige of a high-status person. Even in cases where subordinates may have the knowledge and skill to carry out a task, the relationships between the manager and outsiders might be such that high status would still be required and be desirable.

There is a better answer. Please return to section 42 and make another choice.

55

[from section 66]

YOUR ANSWER: Development of employees will not be accomplished by delegating appraisal of your subordinates.

You are correct.

The only one who can appraise your subordinates effectively is *you*. You must work with employees closely enough so that you will know their strengths and abilities, so you will know what to delegate to them and what not to delegate to them, so you will know in what areas they need to develop in order to reach their individual peak of efficiency.

You are now ready to move on to the next section. In this lesson we have discussed the following questions:

Why do you delegate?

What is delegation?

When do you delegate?

Now we are ready to address ourselves to the question, "How do you delegate?" Turn to section 67 and the beginning of Chapter 3.

YOUR ANSWER: The secretary did not understand the necessity for careful fiscal control. Running the day's totals was one thing Sam could not delegate.

Sam had succumbed to a temptation that faces many executives who come up through the ranks. They are prone to do what they are used to doing, and they avoid undertaking the more complicated management-type tasks (that only they themselves can do).

Patricia was right. An accountant might have done the job even better.

Please return to section 64 and make another choice.

YOUR ANSWER: The best advice to a manager is this: Call on your technical staff to reward and punish employees, once such action seems necessary.

This is not the correct answer.

The process of punishing and rewarding should be kept in the hands of the manager. When sanction-reward systems are given to the staff, the staff cannot help assuming the power and authority of the manager. This dilutes authority and weakens the organization. There is a better answer. Please return to section 51 and make another choice.

YOUR ANSWER: In putting Attlee Baer in charge of the store during his absence, Potts delegated activities which were likely to help Baer develop as a manager.

You are correct. Potts would suffer the consequences and be responsible for whatever happened at the store during his absence. His success would depend upon the success Attlee Baer achieved as acting manager.

Potts, knowingly or unknowingly, was giving Attlee Baer a chance to show what he could do. Baer was getting a chance to learn and a chance to develop. Upon leaving, Potts told Baer that he would have the same authority to make decisions, take action, and give orders as Potts himself. *The manager should delegate activities that will lead to development of subordinates.* It is also possible to delegate in a more limited way, to find out what employees are capable of doing. This principle is illustrated by the following: Rocky Richards was a box boy at Green Front Grocery No. 4. He was competent at his work and seemed anxious to make good. Potts decided to let him try out as a checker during a very slow time of the day. The store manager was:

Delegating a job that probably should be reserved for a more experienced person. **section 43**

Probably testing Rocky's ability to handle greater responsibility.
section 50

59
[*from section 52*]

YOUR ANSWER: Send both the personnel director and the controller. Using two experts will give Sam more information sooner.

This is not correct.

While these two experts could obtain considerable information, they should not be required to report deficiencies of men who are not their subordinates. Almost always, this causes resentment and bad feelings. These assistants should only gather facts and interpret them.

Please return to section 52 and choose another answer.

YOUR ANSWER: Mark should have Sam fire the clerk.

This is hardly the proper function of the top manager.

This is not a hot potato for Sam, nor does it require the position of Sam. Besides, Sam is very busy; he would have to be given all the details of the problem, which would use up his time.

Mark is a manager in his own right and should use rewards and punishments to control his store and exercise leadership.

Please return to section 65 and choose another answer.

YOUR ANSWER: Development of employees will not be accomplished by delegating gradually increasing authority and responsibility.

This is not the expected answer.

Gradually increasing authority and responsibility through the process of delegation is an excellent way to enlarge the skill, ability, and knowledge of an employee. It is therefore an excellent way of developing employees.

In this test question we are discussing the kinds of delegation which should *not* be given.

There is a better answer. Please return to section 66 and make another choice.

YOUR ANSWER: Sam probably was mistaken in not sending his controller to negotiate with the banker for the building loan.

There are some times when an executive should not delegate a task. In this case the controller had the necessary knowledge to negotiate a bank loan and to give the banker the information he needed in order to determine the amount of risk entailed in the loan. Nevertheless, Sam had status in the community. He was a successful businessman, and it is likely that his status would help him negotiate the loan with the banker. The banker might have more confidence in the transaction if he were dealing directly with Sam.

It is possible that you would still like to argue this point, and we would not say absolutely that you are wrong. At the same time, the point that we would like to put across is: on some occasions a manager should not delegate tasks in which his status is required to assure proper execution.

Please go back to section 41 and make another choice.

63

[from section 51]

YOUR ANSWER: The best advice to a manager is this: Never delegate for the purpose of training.

This is not the correct answer.

One major reason for delegating (aside from the fact that it permits the manager to extend himself by getting work done through others) is to develop employees so that they can assume even greater responsibility as time goes on. For this reason we think your answer is incorrect. Please return to section 51 and make another choice.

64

[from section 52]

YOUR ANSWER: Sam should go himself in order to get firsthand knowledge of how the managers are doing and make corrections on the spot.

You are correct.

One of the jobs that a manager should not delegate is the appraisal or correction of his own direct subordinates. In order to be knowledgeable of the work of subordinates, a manager should check on their work personally.

We have now covered two types of activities which only the manager should do and which should not be delegated. These are:

Handling his own hot potatoes.

Appraising his own subordinates.

There are many other occasions on which we have to decide whether or not to delegate. Let's consider some of these situations.

We all like to do the work that we feel most comfortable doing. Every manager must overcome his tendency to do this type of job himself in preference to having it done through others. For example, Sam never got over his love for figures. He habitually ran the day's total on a personal adding machine he kept in his own office. Patricia, his secretary, said, "Why don't you turn that job over to me or to one of the accountants?" In your opinion:

The secretary's suggestion was a good one. In checking the daily totals, Sam was doing detailed work that he should have delegated.   **section 41**

The secretary did not understand the necessity for careful fiscal control. Running the day's totals was one thing Sam could not delegate.

section 56

65
[from section 53]

YOUR ANSWER: Seeing Sam working the early morning produce market, I would say, "There are people in the organization who can do the buying job as well as or better than Sam. Why doesn't he let them do it?"

You would be correct.

A manager cannot possibly maintain the same proficiency in each phase of his work as the employees who do such tasks day after day. The object of extending oneself through delegation is to develop people who can do their jobs effectively and efficiently.

In respect to his activity on the produce market, *Sam was not delegating a job that could be done as well or better by a subordinate.* He did not utilize the specialized skills of the buyers. He was violating a delegation principle.

Rewards and Punishments

In any discussion of what a manager should or should not delegate, consideration must be given to the use of rewards and punishments as a means of exercising control and leadership.

For example, Mark Rathbone, manager of Green Front Grocery No. 2, had a personnel problem. One of the new clerks in his store was completely inaccurate on the cash register, was constantly offending the customers, and was very lazy. Mark decided that the clerk should be fired.

In your opinion what is the best method to fire the clerk?

Mark should fire the clerk himself. **section 40**

Mark should have the personnel director fire the clerk. **section 46**

Mark should have Sam fire the clerk. **section 60**

66
[from section 42]

YOUR ANSWER: You should delegate the tasks and duties that others can handle as well as you.

You are correct.

When other people in your organization can handle certain tasks and duties equally as well as you, you certainly delegate those tasks. As a matter of fact, you actually delegate many things that subordinates *cannot* handle as well as you can, due to insufficient practice or experience on their part. Obviously performance is not going to be at the highest level when employees are undertaking a new task, but the only way people can learn to do some things is by doing them.

Test Question No. 3.

It is generally accepted that delegation is an excellent way to develop employees. This would *not* be accomplished by delegating:

Special projects and assignments that will test the employee's abilities.
section 38

Duties that can be assigned and handled on a temporary basis.
section 49

Appraisal of your subordinates. **section 55**

Gradually increasing authority and responsibility. **section 61**

Chapter 3

HOW DO YOU DELEGATE?

In the preceding lessons we have examined the nature of delegation and the proper times to (and not to) delegate. Now we will consider how to delegate. Here are some ideas to keep in mind as you read this lesson:

1. The objectives of the job being delegated should be clearly understood. State these goals in terms of measurable *results*, not activities.
2. Be sure the subordinate understands the nature and scope of the delegation.
3. Describe the job in writing.
4. Make sure there is agreement with the subordinates on money, men, and materials needed.
5. Assign clear responsibility for the task.
6. Set a target date for completion.
7. Let subordinates do their own thinking.
8. The degree to which one can safely delegate is dependent upon available controls.
9. Set up a system of reporting; then get reports on problems and progress, as well as reports on completion of the task delegated.

Look over these concepts until you feel that you are sufficiently familiar with them.

Setting Objectives

It seems reasonable to assume that we must know what we wish to accomplish before our actions can be directed toward achieving those ends. First, we should state our objectives in terms of *results to be achieved*. Then we should endeavor to develop an understanding of these objectives by those to whom we delegate this work.

Let's consider some specific cases of this principle in action exemplified by Sam and company.

Green Front Grocery Store No. 3 suddenly began to forge ahead in the sale of produce. In fact, their produce sales were far ahead of those in any of the other Green Front outlets. Albert Nicollete was in charge of produce in Store No. 3. He had been told recently by the manager, Charles Shultz, to increase the sales volume of the produce by competitive pricing and vigorous sales methods.

But as sales figures added up it became apparent that Green Front No. 3 sold more produce and made less profit on the transactions than any other Green Front store! Nicollete had underpriced his produce! It was a clear case of misunderstood objectives.

What *was* the objective in this situation?

The objective was to sell more produce. **section 74**

The objective was to sell more produce and thereby increase profits.
section 80

68
[from section 92]

YOUR ANSWER: Wilbur was acting within the nature and scope of the authority delegated by Sam.

At this point we do not have information as to whether the name Tuxedo Street Market would bring in more business or not. We do know that Sam was quite proud of the name, Green Front Grocery, since this was the name of the original market in which he started as a one-man merchandiser.

Remember, Sam did tell Wilbur to run the store as if it were his own. Unfortunately, he did not mean that he could change the entire nature of the business or go so far as to change the name. We have here a case of a lack of understanding on the part of Sam and the person to whom the delegation was made. Wilbur should have been told that certain fundamental matters *are* to be approved by Sam.

Please return to section 92 and make another choice.

69

[*from section 83*]

YOUR ANSWER: Sam had not assigned clear responsibility for the tasks George Gable was undertaking.

There is something to be said for your answer, but it is not the one we would have chosen.

George Gable was told to run the store. But in the process of assigning responsibility, Sam forgot to discuss (and agree upon) the very important matter of men, money, and materials needed to accomplish the tasks which had been delegated.

There is a better answer. Please return to section 83 and make another choice.

70

[*from section 96*]

YOUR ANSWER: Sam needed to be sure that subordinates understood the nature and scope of the delegation.

How could subordinates not understand the nature and scope of the delegation when Sam was overseeing and minutely guiding many of their activities? Sam was oversupervising. Sam had not fully delegated the tasks to his subordinates. He was not using them to the full extent of their capabilities.

Please return to section 96 and make another choice.

71

[*from section 107*]

YOUR ANSWER: Even though you have defined the job, set target dates for completion, and activated reporting systems, you have not done a complete job of delegation unless you have established a system of rewards and punishments.

We do need rewards and punishments in present-day organization, although progress is being made toward other motivating influences which can supersede reward and punishment as the basis of our incentive system. However, among the choices available in this question we believe that you have overlooked the most important. We think it is vital that employees have an understanding of the objectives of the job to be undertaken before they are able to fully comprehend and execute it as you would wish.

Return to section 107 and make another choice.

72
[from section 100]

YOUR ANSWER: After prescribing the goals and objectives of a delegated task, it is a good idea to carefully watch the person to whom we have delegated the job.

Oversupervision or overguiding can destroy the meritorious effects of delegation. One of the principles that the manager should keep in mind is that of letting employees think for themselves.

Oversupervision might lead to destruction of independent thinking.

Please go back to section 100 and make another choice.

73
[from section 79]

YOUR ANSWER: In addition to agreeing on objectives, prescribing the nature and scope of the task, and creating a system of controls on delegated jobs, a manager should work for even greater understanding on the part of the subordinate.

It is true that working for greater understanding on the part of the subordinate is a very desirable and laudable undertaking. But these things must be kept in perspective. One cannot spend all of his time working toward greater understanding. The subordinate has an obligation too. If this sounds as if we are underselling the importance of understanding, then we are misleading you. Understanding is of primary importance.

But if there is agreement on objectives, and if there is agreement on the nature and scope of the task, and if a system of controls on delegated jobs has been created, then we are assuming that a great deal of understanding has been achieved. The thing that is lacking here seems to be the target date or the actual time in which the job can be expected to be completed.

Please return to section 79 and make another choice.

74

[from section 67]

YOUR ANSWER: The objective was to sell more produce.

This is not entirely correct.

It is true that Charles Shultz, the manager of Green Front Store No. 3, had told Nicollete to increase sales volume in the produce. Shultz assumed that Nicollete would know that one of the objectives was to make a profit. Nicollete apparently assumed that it was important to increase the sales volume at the expense of profit, perhaps bringing more customers to the store using produce as a leader. In any case, he misinterpreted his instructions to meet competitive prices.

Please return to section 67 and make another choice.

75

[from section 101]

YOUR ANSWER: The paperback book racks were not installed because Sam had not assigned clear responsibility for the task.

You are correct.

Sam had only mentioned that possibilities of putting in the paperback book racks should be explored. He did not indicate *who* was responsible for doing *what,* nor *when* it should be done. It is important in the process of delegation to be sure that the manager assigns clear responsibility for the execution of the task delegated. (If this responsibility includes completion of the work by a certain date, that should also be specified.)

Here is a related case. Sam and his managers agreed that Green Front Grocery stores should install a new line of frozen food products. New refrigerators were required, so the boxes were ordered by the controller, who worked with Sam at downtown headquarters. Six weeks later, only Store No. 2 had installed the equipment and requested purchase of the frozen food supply.

Why do you suppose the other managers had failed to install frozen food departments?

The communication was too indirect. **section 82**

A target date had not been set for execution of the task. **section 96**

76
[from section 102]

YOUR ANSWER: When delegating to employees to any broad degree, you should give the subordinate complete freedom to act once there is a definite understanding concerning the nature and scope of the job.

It is necessary to have an understanding about the nature and scope of the job, but when delegating broadly this cannot be done in any great detail. In delegating broadly, however, the manager who conveys the delegation should certainly have an adequate set of controls to be sure that the objectives are being achieved.

Please go back to section 102 and make another choice.

77
[from section 92]

YOUR ANSWER: Wilbur was *not* acting within the nature and scope of the authority delegated by Sam.

You are correct.

In discussing the delegation with Wilbur, Sam emphasized profits and customer service, but assumed that the name and major physical characteristics of the store were set and not to be changed. Wilbur, on the other hand, understood that he could run the store "as if it were his own." He did not like the name; he made what he thought was a change for the better.

It seems obvious that Sam did not give Wilbur a proper understanding of the nature and scope of the delegation. The manager must understand his obligation to see that objectives are understood. The task should be clearly described, preferably in writing. It is a good idea to also state the objectives of the delegation in writing.

Let's review; should a proper statement of objectives be more concerned with desirable activities or measurable results?

Desirable activities.　**section 88**

Measurable results.　**section 103**

78
[from section 104]

YOUR ANSWER: All of these are important guidelines to effective delegation: Set up a system which reports problems and progress; delegate to the degree controls are available; resist thinking for the subordinate.

You are correct.

On major jobs we need a system that reports problems and progress. We need to set target dates for the completion of projects. Whenever we delegate we must be sure that adequate management controls are available to determine that standards are being met and that corrective action ensues when they are not. We must also be very careful to resist thinking for the subordinates. Otherwise they will not become the reliable, innovating, creative type of employee we are trying to develop, and it means that we are not extending ourselves through delegation.

In this lesson we have been considering possible answers to the question "How do we delegate?" We have said:

Employees must be given objectives stated in terms of measurable results; objectives and goals of delegated tasks must be both known and understood.

Employees are entitled to know the nature and scope of the delegation; the job is best defined in writing; the responsibility for execution of the task should be clear; a date for completion should be agreed upon.

Let subordinates do their own thinking.

The degree to which one can delegate safely is dependent upon available controls. Controls call for a reporting system that communicates problems and progress and task completion.

Thus far in this lesson we have asked and answered the following questions: "What *is* delegation?" "When do we delegate?" "How do we delegate?"

In the next chapter we shall ask: "To whom do we delegate?" Turn now to section 114 and start Chapter 4.

YOUR ANSWER: After prescribing the goals and objectives of the task, it is a good idea to describe the task in writing.

You are correct.

Prescribing objectives is not easy. Once objectives are understood, it is a very good idea to commit them to writing to serve as a reminder both to the person doing the delegating and to the person receiving the delegation. Other choices you had in answering this question implied that close or continual supervision was needed after delegation has been made. However, oversupervision defeats the purpose of delegation. If employees need training, training should be given; but once a task is delegated, an employee should be left on his own to carry out the task. He should be held accountable for results.

Question No. 3.

In addition to agreeing on objectives, prescribing the nature and scope of the task, and creating a system of controls on delegated jobs, a manager should:

Work for even greater understanding on the part of the subordinate.
section 73

Require interim reports at key points, permitting no further action unless effective progress is assured. **section 87**

Take a forward-looking view in regard to mistakes. **section 97**

Set a target date for completion of the assigned or delegated task.
section 104

80

[from section 67]

YOUR ANSWER: The objective was to sell more produce and thereby increase profits.

You are correct.

Shultz did not give Nicollete a sufficient understanding of the objectives; consequently, Nicollete could not carry out this particular delegation. Nicollete interpreted the instructions as meaning only that produce sales should be increased, perhaps thinking that the difference in profit would be made up on other items.

Misunderstanding objectives can cause misdirected effort. Objectives or goals of the task delegated should be understood. They should be stated in terms of measurable results, rather than as activities.

Our next example involves a notions manufacturing and sales company in which the district manager told the local branch, "Our reason for being in business is to make money. It's as simple as that."

In response to the remark, the head of the local branch conducted a ruthless and unethical high-pressure sales campaign. The outlet made a huge profit; the branch manager was promoted. But the firm in the meantime had lost many friends. At the end of the profitable year, conditions changed for the worse.

Is this another case of a misunderstood objective? Was the objective clearly stated to the local manager?

Yes, the objective was clearly stated. **section 86**

No, the objective was not clearly stated. **section 93**

81

[from section 107]

YOUR ANSWER: Even though you have defined the job, set target dates for completion, and activated reporting systems, you have not done a complete delegation job unless you have followed recognized channels of communication.

Channels of communication and channels of command are not necessarily the same, although in general they overlap. We do think that in this case there is a better answer than the one you have chosen. In delegation, one of the processes we like to follow encourages the person delegating and the person delegated to be in as close communication as possible. But in the instance we now have in front of us, we think that it is more important that the delegator has conveyed an understanding of the objective of the task on which the person will be working.

Go back to section 107 and make another choice.

82

[from section 75]

YOUR ANSWER: The other store managers had failed to install frozen food departments because the communication was too indirect.

This does not seem possible.

In the first place, the store managers had agreed with Sam that such an installation should be made.

The communications were good enough, as far as they went. Certainly they were direct between Sam and his subordinates. The problem seems to be one of not setting up a time by which the equipment and merchandise would be installed.

Go back now to section 75 and try again.

83

[from section 103]

YOUR ANSWER: Put assignments and delegated work into writing.

You are correct.

If Sam had written a memorandum indicating the degree of freedom that Harry and Kenneth had in setting markups, the problem probably would not have occurred.

Here is another instance.

George Gable, the recently hired manager at Green Front Grocery No. 1, had also been told by Sam to run his store as his own. Gable looked over his help situation and decided to hire one more checker and one more produce man. He also increased expenditures for alterations and maintenance; and he requisitioned new supplies, not at the end of the year, but at the end of a six-month period. Naturally, overhead costs went up. This was a great surprise to Sam, who had felt that a year's supplies had already been ordered and set aside for Store No. 1. Which of the following best describes what had happened in this situation?

Sam had not assigned clear responsibility for the tasks George Gable was undertaking. **section 69**

Sam had not set a target date for completion of the jobs. **section 90**

Sam and George had not agreed on the men, money, and materials needed to carry out the delegated job. **section 101**

84

[from section 104]

YOUR ANSWER: All of these are important guidelines to effective delegation: Take a secure view of deviations and differences; set fixed standards of acceptable performance; establish and follow channels of communication.

Generally, the secure executive delegates best, but it is not always wise to be too secure about deviations and differences. In general, standards are not always the best standards. Following channels of communication is certainly desirable most of the time, but channels of communication should remain open, and if blockages occur, steps should be taken to establish alternate routes.

So the guidelines given in the statement that you chose are only partially true and there is a better answer. Please return to section 104 and make another choice.

85

[from section 100]

YOUR ANSWER: After prescribing the goals and objectives of a delegated task, it is a good idea to employ minimum standards as criteria of excellence of performance.

This is not the answer we expected.

Standards of performance are useful in certain phases of management control, but the statement is too general to be very useful here.

We are interested in the step which follows the prescribing of the goals and objectives. One thing we have learned in this lesson is that objectives are not only hard to reach, they are hard to remember. Please return to section 100 and make another choice.

86

[from section 80]

YOUR ANSWER: Yes, the objective was clearly stated.

The district manager was being dramatic but inaccurate when he said, "Our reason for being in business is to make money, it's as simple as that." Present-day managers must understand there are more than mere profit objectives.

The district manager oversimplified the situation. Whether for this reason or some other, the head of the local branch conducted the kind of sales campaign that lost the company many friends and was in the long run harmful to business. Certainly he did not understand the overall company objectives.

Please go back to section 80 and make another choice.

87

[from section 79]

YOUR ANSWER: In addition to agreeing on objectives, prescribing the nature and scope of the task, and creating a system of controls on delegated jobs, a manager should require interim reports at key points, permitting no further action unless effective progress is assured.

There are a number of instances where interim or progress reports are vital. This is particularly true of a long-range project that requires the work of many people for completion. But herein also lies a trap. The manager can spend so much time checking intermediate reports that he makes all of the decisions for the subordinate. This means he has not truly delegated. In general, it is well for the manager to hold employees responsible for results. He should not review decisions, but should review results.

In this case we think the factor that is missing is agreement on the date when the delegated task or project should be completed.

Please go back to section 79 and make another choice.

88

[from section 77]

YOUR ANSWER: A proper statement of objectives should be more concerned with desirable activities.

You are mistaken.

These days there is much concern over management by objectives, but organizations frequently make the mistake of stating their objectives in broad and unmeasurable terms. This means that statements of objectives often tend to become rather platitudinous, high-sounding statements of principles or philosophies and cannot serve as proper guides to the organizational activities. Consequently, organizations cannot know for sure whether they ever achieve their objectives.

No, objectives should be stated in terms of expected results. This is a very important point. You will understand delegation better if you understand how to state them.

Go back to section 77.

89

[from section 101]

YOUR ANSWER: The paperback book racks were not installed because Sam was resisting thinking for his employees.

This is not the correct answer.

As a matter of fact, the suggestion had been Sam's, and, apparently, had been ignored, resisted, or forgotten by the store managers. We have no evidence that Sam hovered over his store managers making their decisions for them.

We have evidence of other mismanagement in the delegating process, but this is a good point to remember: If a person is delegating a job, he should delegate the whole job and resist thinking for his employees. But our question involves a different problem.

It seems to us that the problem here was that Sam had merely mentioned the idea of installing paperback book racks as being a good idea and had not assigned direct and clear responsibility for execution of the task.

Please go back to section 101 and choose again.

90
[from section 83]

YOUR ANSWER: Sam had not set a target date for completion of the jobs.

This is not the correct answer.

There were several target dates that might have been set, but the delegation happened to be for the management of a continuous operation of the store.

This brings up a good point, however. It is very important that the person doing the delegating agree with the person receiving the delegation upon any target dates which may be necessary.

We think the problem here, however, has to do with reaching an understanding on the men, money, and materials available to carry out the expected tasks.

Return now to section 83 and make another choice.

91
[from section 102]

YOUR ANSWER: When delegating to employees to any broad degree, you should set up adequate management controls, which set standards, check on results, and correct deviations.

You are absolutely right!

While it is important to convey to those receiving the delegation the full nature and scope of the job, any broad delegation must by all means be accompanied by effective management controls. Management controls set standards, check on results, and correct deviations. These are a vital accompaniment to delegation. This means, among other things, that a system of reporting achievement of objectives must be developed.

Let's consider another such case.

Harry Quint's Green Front Grocery No. 5 was located in the suburban Moondown area. The store had opened almost simultaneously with the subdivision, and as the community grew, business grew. Profits climbed gradually. One day, though, Sam was surprised to find out that a small competitor was enlarging his store; it turned out that the seemingly small operation was actually doing about twice the business of the larger and more elaborate Green Front Grocery. Sam immediately went looking for the reasons and soon determined that at Green Front No. 5 some rudeness had been experienced by customers, the dairy boxes were frequently dirty, and in general the housekeeping was not up to the standard Sam felt he should expect.

Sam himself had already been vaguely aware of these problems and had asked Quint to correct them. He had assumed that something had been done. The competitor had profited by the failure of Harry Quint to carry out his delegated responsibilities. This would not have happened if Sam had:

A system of reporting on problems and progress. **section 106**

Direct communications. **section 112**

92
[from section 105]

YOUR ANSWER: The expectation of increasing sales and profits by 10 per cent during the coming year is a proper statement of objectives because it refers to expected results.

You are correct.

A 10 per cent increase is measurable, which means that you can determine whether or not you have achieved the objective.

It is most helpful to state objectives in terms of achievable results, and it is very important in delegating to subordinates that objectives be properly stated and mutually understood. Otherwise subordinates will make erroneous assumptions.

For instance, Wilbur Potts was energetic, and eager to improve his operation. He was pleased when Sam said, "I want you to run the store as if it were your own. Show me a profit. Keep the customers; but other than that, how you do this is your business." Wilbur gave the matter a good deal of thought. One of the things about which he was concerned was the name. He did not think *Green Front Grocery* was a good name. He thought other names would have more customer appeal. He repainted the store front and renamed the store *Tuxedo Street Market*.

How do you feel about Wilbur's action?

Wilbur was acting within the nature and scope of the authority delegated by Sam. **section 68**

Wilbur was *not* acting within the nature and scope of the authority delegated by Sam. **section 77**

93
[from section 80]

YOUR ANSWER: No, the objective was *not* clearly stated.

You are correct.

This statement is made frequently: "Our objective is to make money." It is of course true that one of the objectives of any profit-making concern is making a profit. But there are many other objectives. In this case, the local manager definitely did not understand total company objectives.

The determination of objectives is an important function of the manager. We have seen that objectives should be stated in terms of expected results, rather than in terms of activities. When Sam told his Green Front Grocery store managers that he expected every employee in the Green Front chain to work toward improved customer service, was he stating the objective in terms of *expected results* or *desirable activities*?

Expected results. **section 99**

Desirable activities. **section 105**

94

[from section 107]

YOUR ANSWER: Even though you have defined the job, set target dates for completion, and activated reporting systems, you have not done a complete delegation job unless you have provided flexibility in completion dates.

No, you are wrong.

One of the principles of delegation is to set target dates so that the person who is required to perform the task will know when he is expected to finish. It is further necessary that the person doing the delegating know something about how much progress is being made in the work. But here we are talking about a different thing altogether. We think that it is very important for the person receiving the delegation to have an understanding of the goals and objectives which are to be achieved through his execution of the task that has been delegated. Turn to section 107 again and make another choice.

95

[from section 104]

YOUR ANSWER: All of these are important guidelines to effective delegation: Assist in step-by-step execution of the task; work for even greater understanding of the job by the employee; establish a fair system of rewards and punishments.

This is not the best set of guidelines for delegation.

For instance, we would take issue with the guiding statement that asks us to assist in step-by-step execution of the task.

This is almost the opposite of good practice in delegating work. If we are to assist step by step, the person to whom the job is delegated never develops the degree of independence required and is held responsible not for results but for the way he goes about achieving results.

Within reason, we should certainly work to achieve greater understanding of the job by the employee.

Until we become more adept at management, we will probably use a system of rewards and punishments, although we should be striving for self-motivation where accomplishment is its own reward. If we have rewards and punishments, they should certainly be fair.

While some of the guidelines given in this paragraph are true, they are not universally true, and there is another paragraph that contains better answers. Please return to section 104 and make another choice.

YOUR ANSWER: The other store managers had failed to install frozen food departments because a target date had not been set for execution of the task.

You are correct.

It is essential that the person who delegates the task and the person to whom the task is delegated have a mutual understanding of the target date—the date on which the assigned tasks should be completed. It is also important that communications should be as direct as possible between boss and subordinate; the more intervening assistants there are in the chain, the more likely it is that the understanding of what is to be done will be distorted.

Establishing Controls

Early in the history of Green Front Groceries, soon after the opening of the second store, Sam spent his time fairly evenly between the two stores. When he visited either of the stores, he nearly always suggested new ways of doing things, persuading managers to modify their decisions and guiding them in directions that seemed to him to be desirable. What would you say about Sam's actions?

Sam needed to be sure that the subordinates understood the nature and scope of the delegation. **section 70**

Sam did not let his subordinates think for themselves. **section 102**

Sam knew that the degree to which one can successfully delegate depends upon management controls that are available. **section 113**

97

[*from section 79*]

YOUR ANSWER: In addition to agreeing on objectives, prescribing the nature and scope of the task, and creating a system of controls on delegated jobs, a manager should take a forward-looking view in regard to mistakes.

In this lesson, from time to time, we will make the statement, "You cannot control the past." This might lead you to believe that it is well to take a forward-looking view in regard to mistakes. The forward-looking view should certainly be to avoid foreseeable mistakes. In delegation, we must be willing to accept the risk of mistakes on the part of subordinates. This does not mean that we encourage mistakes. It does mean that we try to avoid a condition where the fear of making mistakes prevents the person to whom we have delegated from making decisions and taking action.

In the question you are answering, however, there is a point that seems to us to be a good deal more important. This is the factor regulating the date of completion. In any delegation, target dates are most important.

Please go back to section 79 and make another choice.

98

[*from section 105*]

YOUR ANSWER: The expectation of increasing sales and profits by 10 per cent during the coming year is a proper statement of objectives because it refers to desirable activities.

There is a better answer.

It is essential in delegation that both superior and subordinate understand objectives, and that these objectives be stated in terms of measurable results rather than in terms of desirable activities. It will still be necessary for those receiving the delegation to figure out how to achieve the objectives and what activities will be necessary in order to obtain the 10 per cent increase, but before they do this they need to understand their goals.

Go back now to section 105 and make another choice.

YOUR ANSWER: When Sam told his store managers to work toward improved customer service, he was stating the objective in terms of expected results.

Not exactly.

Sam stated his objective in terms of activities rather than results. Working toward improved customer service is a laudable *activity,* but the form of that improvement—when, how, and how much— was not stated.

There is a better answer. Please return to section 93 and make another choice.

YOUR ANSWER: Even though you have defined the job, set target dates for completion, and activated reporting systems, you have not done a complete delegation job unless you have conveyed an understanding of the goals of the task to be undertaken.

You are correct.

In delegating to subordinates, one of the major considerations of the manager should be conveying an understanding of the goals and objectives to be achieved through execution of the delegated task. Rewards and punishments, effective channels of communication, and target dates are all very important in a work system. These have all been discussed in the lesson. But they must take second place in importance to the establishing of objectives.

Question No. 2.

After prescribing the goals and objectives of a delegated task, it is a good idea to:

Carefully watch the person to whom we have delegated the job.
section 72

Describe the task in writing. **section 79**

Employ minimum standards as criteria of excellence of performance.
section 85

Help the employee step by step as he performs the task. **section 108**

101
[from section 83]

YOUR ANSWER: Sam and George had not agreed upon the men,
money, and materials needed to carry out the delegated job.

You are correct.

Sam had apparently made the assumption that the expenditures
of men, money, and materials would continue the same as in the
past. George made the assumption that he could increase or de-
crease them as he saw fit. Sam and George had not agreed on the
number of men that should be hired in the store, the amount of
money that should be expended on such things as alterations and
maintenance, and the materials and supplies that would be needed
to operate the enterprise.

Assigning Responsibility and Setting Target Dates

As is common in well-run enterprises, Sam held frequent meet-
ings of his managers. At one of these he said, "I think one of you
ought to investigate the possibilities of putting in paperback book
racks in your stores."

Six months later nothing had happened. Why?

Sam had not assigned clear responsibility for the task. **section 75**

Sam was resisting thinking for his employees. **section 89**

Sam had not made his communication as direct as possible.
section 109

YOUR ANSWER: Sam did not let his subordinates think for themselves.

You are correct.

He was inspecting minutely the moves of his managers and other subordinates; in fact, he seemed to be doing their thinking for them. This meant that they could not develop themselves, that their initiative was not being utilized, that they were not becoming more valuable employees, and that Sam was not using *his* abilities to accomplish management functions. In other words, he was not sufficiently extending himself. So, here is a rule:

Resist thinking for your subordinates.

The success of delegation often rests on the effectiveness of controls.

Here is an illustration from the annals of the Green Front Grocery chain.

When Charlie Conoway first joined the Green Front chain as controller, he was appalled by the lack of system in the books.

"You ask young managers to take over the stores and to run them as if they were their own. You really delegate quite broadly. Yet you don't know where the money goes, why it goes, and for what it goes."

When delegating to employees to any broad degree, you should:

Give the subordinate complete freedom to act once there is a definite understanding concerning the nature and scope of the job. **section 76**

Set up adequate management controls, which set standards, check on results, and correct deviations. **section 91**

103
[from section 77]

YOUR ANSWER: A proper statement of objectives should be more concerned with measurable results.

You are correct.

An objective tells us where we wish to go—the goal we wish to reach. Saying that we are working *toward* something, or believing that *something* should be done, is not a proper statement of a goal. A goal should be stated in terms of measurable results, such as measurable changes in total sales, profits, inventory, or production.

In any case, a serious effort should be made to state the goal in some measurable terms. This does not have to be a monetary or mathematical measure; almost anything will suffice that can be recognized when it happens. When objectives are so stated, delegations can be made, preferably in writing, that indicate clearly the areas of responsibility and authority.

In talking to Harry Quint, the manager of Green Front Grocery No. 5, and to his produce manager, Kenneth Ambrose, Sam discussed the markup on produce. Normally, Green Front set a 35 per cent markup. Sam thought that this could safely be lowered for a period of time in order to meet competition. He had it in mind to set a 25 per cent markup in place of the usual 35 per cent.

A week later there was trouble. In putting the instructions into effect, Harry and Kenneth had set a 20 per cent markup. When Sam found this out, he demanded an explanation. Harry insisted that Sam had said 20 per cent would be sufficient. Kenneth was not sure, but went along with Harry. Sam said they were both wrong. Tempers flared.

But this could have been avoided quite simply. What would be your advice?

Put assignments and delegated work into writing. **section 83**

Insist that subordinates put the results of all conferences into written form and send you a file copy for confirmation. **section 110**

YOUR ANSWER: In addition to agreeing on objectives, prescribing the nature and scope of the task, and creating a system of controls on delegated jobs, a manager should set a target date for completion of the assigned or delegated task.

You are correct.

A frequent omission in making assignments or delegating jobs is failure to agree with the subordinate on the time in which he is expected to complete the job given.

While it is important to develop understandings about major long-term projects and to set up a system of interim reporting, and while it is important to exercise some tolerance toward inevitable mistakes in order to create the kind of climate in which subordinates feel free to act, the most important response to the question which you have been answering is *to set a definite target date for the completion of the delegated task.*

Question No. 4.

The four paragraphs below set forth guidelines for executive action. In which paragraph are *all* of the guidelines important to effective delegation?

Set up a system which reports problems and progress; delegate to the degree controls are available; resist thinking for the subordinate.
section 78

Take a secure view of deviations and differences; set fixed standards of acceptable performance; establish and follow channels of communication. **section 84**

Assist in step-by-step execution of the task; work for even greater understanding of the job by the employee; establish a fair system of rewards and punishments. **section 95**

Provide considerable flexibility with regard to completion dates.
section 111

105

[from section 93]

YOUR ANSWER: When Sam told his store managers to work toward improved customer service, he was stating the objective in terms of desirable activities.

You are correct.

However, Sam was making a mistake by stating objectives in this way. He should have couched his instructions in terms of measurable end results, such as faster check-out, free delivery, telephone order service, or more clearly marked prices.

The following week, Sam stated that he expected sales and profits to increase by 10 per cent in the coming year. Why is this a proper statement of objectives?

This is a proper statement of objectives because it refers to expected results. **section 92**

This is a proper statement of objectives because it refers to desirable activities. **section 98**

106

[from section 91]

YOUR ANSWER: The competitor had profited by the failure of Harry Quint to carry out his delegated responsibilities. This would not have happened if Sam had a system of reporting on problems and progress.

You are quite correct.

Sam had talked to Harry Quint, had been aware of the problem, and had assumed that the things needing correction would be corrected. This is where he went astray. There was no system by which Harry reported back to him on problems occurring in the store and neighborhood, or upon the progress being made on the tasks delegated. In delegating it is most important to set up a system of reporting: report problems and progress; report completion.

Now you are ready for the Test Sequence. Go on to section 107.

TEST

Question No. 1.

You may define the job, set target dates for completion, and activate reporting systems, but you have not done a complete job of delegation unless you have:

Established a system of rewards and punishments. **section 71**

Followed recognized channels of communication. **section 81**

Provided flexibility in completion dates. **section 94**

Conveyed an understanding of the goals of the task to be undertaken. **section 100**

YOUR ANSWER: After prescribing the goals and objectives of a delegated task, it is a good idea to help the employee step by step as he performs the task.

There is not much point in delegating if you are going to continue to help the employee step by step. It is important that you learn to delegate the whole package. If the employee needs to be trained to do the job, for goodness' sake train him! But do not hover over him and do not do his thinking for him.

Here we are interested in taking the next step beyond the prescribing of goals and objectives. One thing we have learned in this lesson is that objectives are often forgotten. Please go back to section 100 and make another choice.

109

[from section 101]

YOUR ANSWER: The paperback book racks were not installed because Sam had not made his communications as direct as possible.

Quite the contrary.

Sam made a face-to-face communication to his store managers. This is about as direct as communication can get.

Sam had simply mentioned that the idea of putting in paperback book racks should be explored and that managers should investigate the possibilities involved. He did not make a direct assignment nor did he have an understanding with the men concerning the project.

Go back to section 101 and make another choice.

110

[from section 103]

YOUR ANSWER: Insist that subordinates put the results of all conferences into written form and send you a file copy for confirmation.

This is one way of doing it, and it might have the desired results. But it has two major drawbacks. First, being a busy executive, Sam might not get around to reading the memo until after the program had gone into effect, thereby rendering the memo useless. More important, this method places the responsibility on the subordinates rather than the boss. Communication is the boss's responsibility.

Sam thought he was quite clear in indicating the percentage of markup that was satisfactory to him. He thought he had delegated quite clearly the degree to which Kenneth had freedom in pricing his vegetables. On the other hand, Harry and Kenneth felt that Sam had indicated freedom up to a 20 per cent markup. The problem was one of understanding.

We think, perhaps, this might have been avoided if Sam could have put his thinking into writing. It is better that the manager do the thinking rather than the subordinate.

Please return to section 103 and make another choice.

YOUR ANSWER: This is an important guideline to effective delegation: Provide considerable flexibility concerning completion dates.

This is not the best answer.

Sometimes flexible completion dates are desirable; more often than not it is better to set a firm date for completion of a job or project. All of us have an inclination to meet definite goals and deadlines and to ignore more loosely defined targets.

There is a much better answer. Please go back to section 104 and make another choice.

YOUR ANSWER: The competitor had profited by the failure of Harry Quint to carry out his delegated responsibilities. This would not have happened if Sam had direct communications.

This is not the correct answer.

Sam and Harry had been in direct communication. Sam had been aware of the problem. Sam had discussed the problem with Harry Quint. The failure seems to be that Harry Quint had not corrected any of the problems enumerated. The clerks were still rude, the dairy boxes still dirty, the housekeeping not up to standard. If reports of progress had been made the situation might have been corrected.

Please return to section 91 and pick another answer.

YOUR ANSWER: Sam knew that the degree to which one can successfully delegate depends upon management controls that are available.

Your answer is partially true. However, Sam was not using management controls; he was hovering over employees, inspecting everything they did. In so doing, he was not permitting them to think for themselves, nor was he permitting himself to fill all of the functions a manager needs to fill. (Fortunately we are told that Sam learned better as time went on.)

There is a more appropriate answer. Please go back to section 96 and make another choice.

Chapter 4

TO WHOM DO YOU DELEGATE?

This lesson will be devoted to finding answers to the question "To whom do you delegate?" We will be covering these points:

Delegate to *your* immediate subordinates (not to *their* subordinates).

Avoid the obvious. Do not give in to the temptation to delegate to the most capable.

Delegate to persons with the most unused time.

Delegate to the person who needs the experience.

Delegate to the person whose ability you wish to test.

Delegate to the lowest level at which performance capability exists.

When you feel you are familiar with these concepts, go on with the lesson.

Let's leave Sam and his Green Front stores for a moment in order to consider the problems of delegation encountered in a much larger and more complex organization. Specifically, we're going to refer to the administrative department of a large Atlantic seaboard state.

When Hurricane Jessie hit the coast, it caused extensive damage throughout the state. The Governor called an emergency session of the Legislature. He asked that the Board of Control formulate a plan to take care of the disaster areas.

The Board of Control met with the Director, Deputy Director, and Chief Budget Analyst of the Department of Fiscal Review.

Governor
Board of Control
Director
Deputy Director
Chief Budget Analyst
Section A   Section B   Section C   Section D   Section E

Following this meeting, the Director of Fiscal Review assigned to Section C of his department the responsibility for making a study.

69

After the Director of Fiscal Review had assigned the hurricane damage survey to Section C, the Section C analyst started the investigation. But as the work proceeded, the lower house of the Legislature tended to interfere. Members of the Finance Committee (especially the Chairman) reviewed and revised the drafts of the plan. Within the Board of Control itself there was disagreement.

The Governor, realizing that delay could be disastrous, called a meeting in his office with the analyst from Section C and Chairman of the Finance Committee of the lower house; he directed that the analyst take certain action.

After that, the work progressed more smoothly. The Governor and the Finance Committee Chairman were satisfied. But the Board of Control was understandably upset; the Director, the Assistant Director, and the Chief Budget Analyst were concerned by the outcome; and the Section C analyst himself was quite uncomfortable.

What is your reaction? Was the Governor delegating correctly or incorrectly in this instance?

Correctly; he was delegating to a direct subordinate. **section 120**

Incorrectly; he was delegating around (bypassing) the levels of command. **section 127**

Correctly; he was delegating to the person who most needed the experience. **section 134**

115
[from section 132]

YOUR ANSWER: McGowan wanted to develop his subordinates.

You are correct.

We delegate for a number of reasons. Primarily, we delegate to extend ourselves. But we also delegate to develop people, so that they will become more valuable and able to take on increasing responsibility.

Let's consider another facet of delegation. The Chief Budget Analyst knew that there would soon be an opening for a promotion to senior analyst in the division. Al, one of the Grade III analysts, had been through the mill; Al was a good man, but not outstanding. Joe, another Grade III, seemed to be outstanding, but was untried. At this time a difficult assignment, which required dealing with the Legislature, came to the Budget Division. The Chief Budget Analyst decided to see how good Joe was. He gave Joe the assignment.

How do you feel about this delegation? We know that one reason for delegating is to test the abilities of subordinates. But what *sort* of tasks should one delegate?

Delegate new and difficult tasks. **section 123**

Delegate only those tasks he knows how to do. **section 148**

YOUR ANSWER: The manager should delegate to a person whose ability he wishes to test.

You are correct.

From time to time to assess the abilities of a person and feel that he is capable of more difficult tasks than those to which he has heretofore been assigned. At this point, by proper delegation we can determine whether or not the subordinate has the capacity for more difficult jobs. And we should always keep in mind that everyone gains when we encourage lower level employees to take on more authority and responsibility: They gain in skills, and the company gets more work per wage dollar.

Let's add another consideration to our list:

1. Delegate only to immediate subordinates.
2. Avoid the obvious.
3. Consider delegating to the person with the most unused time.
4. Delegate to the person who needs experience.
5. Delegate to the person whose ability one would like to test.
6. Delegate, or encourage delegation, to the person:

Who has the higher status and authority. **section 126**

Who is at the lowest organizational level at which performance capability exists. **section 137**

117

[from section 145]

YOUR ANSWER: The Budget Chief was delegating to the unit that had the greatest available free time.

You are correct.

Section C was overloaded, but Section D seemed to have time to do a job of the magnitude suggested by the Governor.

It is a good practice to delegate to the person who has the greatest amount of available time. This equalizes the workload and sometimes increases the ability of people to produce.

On rare occasions it is desirable to "delegate to weakness," because experience sometimes builds strength. It is always good business to delegate to the lowest level at which there is a capability to do the job. (We mention this in passing. In the case we are discussing, this was not an issue.)

The staff of Budget Section D was pleased. Previously there had been complaints that "the boss gives all the big ones to Section C."

But the boss was not quite so pleased. As a matter of fact, he was worried. He knew that the staff in Section C would have delivered even though they were overloaded. He was not so sure that Section D had sufficient capability to produce an answer to such a complex problem in the required time.

How do you feel about this situation?

The Chief Budget Analyst was taking an unwarranted chance by delegating to the section he wanted to test. **section 124**

The Chief Budget Analyst was avoiding the obvious; he was giving others the needed opportunity. **section 132**

The Chief Budget Analyst was delegating to the lowest level of responsibility. **section 143**

YOUR ANSWER: A manager should always delegate to his immediate subordinate and should never discuss the task delegated with any other than his immediate subordinate.

This is not correct.

Traditional management precepts indicate that the chain of command should always be observed. In practice this may not be realistic, but good business practice demands that we delegate only to subordinates, although we may *communicate* to those who will be affected by the action. Many times we delegate to one person but communicate to a number of people other than those to whom the delegation has been made. Frequently we consult others than the person to whom we delegate so that we have valid information which will enable us to delegate in a more reasonable fashion.

Please return to section 128 and make another choice.

YOUR ANSWER: Saying that the manager should delegate tasks to the lowest level of competence and at the same time saying he should delegate only to the persons who are his immediate subordinates indicates that management theory is inconsistent. A manager might have a difficult time doing both.

The thesis of this lesson is that managers should delegate only to their immediate subordinates and also that tasks should be delegated to the lowest level of the organization at which capability to perform such tasks exists. This means that each manager is obligated to delegate to his subordinate those tasks which it is appropriate for them to perform. It does not mean that the president of a company should delegate personally to a person much lower in the management hierarchy. Please go back to section 138 and make another choice.

120

[*from section 114*]

YOUR ANSWER: The Governor was delegating correctly; he was delegating to a direct subordinate.

The analyst in Section C is organizationally far removed from the Governor. The delegation in this case becomes quite complex because of the numerous levels of command involved.

There is a better answer. Please return to section 114 and pick it.

121

[*from section 141*]

YOUR ANSWER: Some good rules of delegation are:

1. One should delegate only to immediate subordinates.
2. One should avoid the obvious.
3. One should delegate to persons with the most unused time.

You are correct.

Persons who are most experienced at taking on new tasks are frequently also the busiest. Persons with unused time should be given an opportunity to fill such time with useful and significant work. Their lack of experience weighs against their greater availability, but the fact that they are being given an opportunity to gain new experience and develop at their job tends to tip the scales in their favor.

Ralph Hickman decided there was another good reason for having Matty Gibb head up the Atom Liner Guides Company task force on reorganization. He arrived at this position because one should:

1. Delegate only to immediate subordinates.
2. Avoid the obvious.
3. Delegate to the person having the most time.
4.

Choose the appropriate rule to fill the blank after Number 4.

Delegate to the person who needs experience. **section 129**

Delegate to the person who has seniority. **section 142**

122
[from section 140]

YOUR ANSWER: Ways of delegating work may become habitual. For this reason it is a good idea to do the job yourself until you feel you know it; then delegate.

This is not the correct answer.

The manager has far too much to do; he cannot take time to learn every job that he is called upon to supervise. He needs to know how well work is being performed, but this is the job that is done when he establishes effective management controls. As we have said before, effective management controls should accompany all delegation.

But it is possible to form a habit of delegating to certain people. We may overload some and completely overlook the availability and capability of others within the organization. For this reason, it is a good idea to consider different ways of accomplishing delegation and to consider different people for tasks that are normally assigned to one or two individuals.

Please go back to section 140 and make another choice.

123
[from section 115]

YOUR ANSWER: To test the abilities of a subordinate, one should delegate new and difficult tasks.

You are correct.

Joe appeared to have everything necessary to assure his success as a senior analyst, but as a Grade III he was untried in some of the situations he would be required to meet as a senior. The Chief Budget Analyst can try to discover Joe's capabilities by assigning him to tasks of increasing difficulty.

It is a good idea to delegate to a person you wish to test. This does not mean we keep people from operating in their specialties. For the most part we assign subordinates to those things they do best, but we do not let them get in a rut.

One of the major public works projects in the state was the construction of the South Aqueduct. The Governor knew that the funding of the South Aqueduct was in for close scrutiny by an interim committee of the Legislature; he asked the Board of Control to recommend an expert to testify on the project.

The Board of Control asked the Chief Budget Analyst to make a recommendation. The Chief Budget Analyst knew that Alvin Linden, a Grade III budget analyst, had thoroughly studied the situation and knew all the technical problems connected with the funding of the project. The Chief Budget Analyst knew something about the situation, but he realized that he did not know as much as Alvin Linden.

In this case the Chief Budget Analyst should recommend Alvin Linden because:

Some jobs requiring thorough knowledge of a situation should be delegated to the lowest possible level at which capability of performing the task exists. **section 135**

You should never stick your own neck out unless you have to.

section 150

124

[from section 117]

YOUR ANSWER: The Chief Budget Analyst was taking an unwarranted chance by delegating to the section he wanted to test.

The Chief Budget Analyst was taking a chance. Whether or not it was an *unwarranted* chance we do not know. We know that he had some doubts about his decision, but he was avoiding the obvious, and he was giving other people in his organization needed opportunities. He was avoiding habitual thinking. In the long run, delegation of this kind pays off if it is accompanied by effective management controls and effective training.

Please return to section 117 and make another choice.

YOUR ANSWER: McGowan was against specialization by his analysts.

We are not arguing against specialization. Specialists are needed and will be needed even more in the future than at present. The question a manager must ask himself is whether the person specializing is indeed a specialist, or merely a generalist who is given routine or specialized tasks. If the specialty is one that cannot lead to a future for the man, the organization owes him a wider breadth of experience so that he can develop and learn other skills. This is good both for the organization and for the man.

Please return to section 132 and make another choice.

YOUR ANSWER: Delegate, or encourage delegation, to the person who has the higher status and authority.

This is not the correct answer.

In delegation we should make an effort to obtain maximum use of abilities at all levels. We should usually delegate to a level in the organization at which performance capability exists and at which the job can be accomplished most effectively and efficiently.

Please go back to section 116 and make another choice.

YOUR ANSWER: The Governor was incorrectly delegating; he was delegating around (bypassing) the levels of command.

You are correct.

The Governor and the Chairman of the Legislative Committee of the lower house were actually delegating to other people's subordinates. This violates an important principle of delegation.

The Governor and the Chairman felt that they needed to communicate directly with the person who was doing the work. Their action, however, as well as the assignment arising from it, bypassed several levels of the organization. This could only lead to future trouble, even though it might be a solution to the immediate problem.

Once this contretemps had passed, the Governor had other experiences with the process of delegation. Here is one.

The Governor told the Chairman of the Board of Control that he wanted the help of a budget analyst in dealing with problems arising from a new social welfare proposal. He indicated that he did not want to stir up the organization again by ignoring the chain of command, as he had during the Hurricane Jessie disaster. He did feel, however, that he should talk directly to the budget analyst about the problem in order to be certain that the assignment was clearly understood. He asked the Chairman to come to his office with the analyst and all other persons who might be involved with the problem.

How was the Governor handling delegation in this case?

The Governor was delegating to a person other than an immediate subordinate. **section 136**

The Governor was delegating to an immediate subordinate, but communicating directly with the one who would do the work. **section 145**

128
[from section 135]

YOUR ANSWER: Good advice to Ralph Hickman, who had bypassed his floor foreman to delegate directly to the chief of Assembly Section 23, would be: When you delegate, delegate to your immediate subordinate, not to your subordinate's subordinate.

You are correct.

On rare occasions we may violate the chain of command in the interest of efficiency and good communication, but delegation is not such an occasion.

We delegate only to our own immediate subordinates. They, in turn, delegate to persons who work for them. We may suggest or even, under certain circumstances, force such delegation, but the delegation is still from our subordinates to their subordinates, not from us to their subordinates.

If the assignment is complex, the *communication* can be made directly to the person who will actually do the work, provided his superiors are present.

We expect our subordinates to delegate to the person who knows the job best. We expect them to select persons who are not busy, who need development, who need testing, or who for some other reason seem to be the appropriate persons to receive the delegation. It is sometimes difficult to avoid the obvious. Often we delegate out of habit.

Atom Liner Guides was the kind of a company that experienced crisis after crisis and rush after rush. Matty Gibb, for example, had another rush job that needed to be absorbed and expedited. He normally would have given this job to Section 12. Now, however, he remembered that in choosing the person to whom one delegates, a manager:

1. Should always delegate to his immediate subordinate.
2. _____

Which of the following paragraphs belongs in the space above?

Should never discuss the task delegated with any other than his immediate subordinate. **section 118**

Should avoid the obvious. He should consider other persons than the one to whom it has become habitual to delegate. **section 141**

129
[from section 121]

YOUR ANSWER: One should:

1. Delegate only to immediate subordinates.
2. Avoid the obvious.
3. Delegate to the person having the most time.
4. Delegate to the person who needs experience.

You are correct.

We frequently delegate to the less experienced person; this gives him needed experience and gives us a chance to see what he can do. This is often more important than delegating to a person who has seniority in the organization. However, it is reasonable to delegate to persons with seniority when other factors are equal or when management has no choice in the matter (due to organizational contracts or other reasons).

Of course there are factors other than experience and availability to be considered when one is looking for the person to whom he should delegate. There is some degree of truth in both of the statements below, but one of the statements is "better" than the other. Which statement is the better one?

The manager should delegate to a person whose ability he wishes to test. **section 116**

The manager should delegate to a person who most needs to develop his skills. **section 153**

130
[from section 138]

YOUR ANSWER: Saying that the manager should delegate tasks to the lowest level of competence, and that the manager should delegate only to persons who are his immediate subordinates, means that the manager must choose between one theory or the other.

While it might seem that there is a conflict between the two statements, in reality this is not so. In this section of the lesson on delegation we have said that the manager should delegate only to his own subordinates. He should never delegate to his subordinate's subordinate. This does not preclude his own subordinate from delegating the task even further down the line. As a matter of fact, each manager should delegate tasks that can be handled better by lower levels of the organization.

Please go back to section 138 and try again.

131
[from section 151]

YOUR ANSWER: I disagree that it is sometimes desirable to delegate a task to a person whose ability you wish to test, even though more capable employees are available for the assignment.

We think you are wrong.

We have learned in this section that there are many factors which should be considered when we try to decide to whom we should delegate. One of these factors is the possibility of testing the capabilities of the subordinate by delegating a task to him that he has not previously handled. Sometimes there is no other way to determine the readiness of an employee to move ahead.

Please return to section 151 and make another choice.

132

[from section 117]

YOUR ANSWER: The Chief Budget Analyst was avoiding the obvious; he was giving others the needed opportunity.

You are correct.

There were risks involved in delegating to Section D; but he had relied too much on Section C in the past, and most of the competence seemed to be building up in that section. It was necessary to take risks so that others could be given opportunities. In spite of the risks, it is good practice to use the process of delegation to create opportunities for developing subordinates.

In another of the sections, Senior Budget Analyst McGowan was in charge of three Grade III budget analysts. One of these analysts had specialized in a narrow field of grants-in-aid programs; although the man had become quite a specialist in this field, McGowan felt that he needed broadening. Therefore, McGowan began to delegate other kinds of studies and analyses for this particular analyst to work on.

What was McGowan's motive in this case?

McGowan wanted to develop his subordinates. **section 115**

McGowan was against specialization by analysts. **section 125**

133

[from section 140]

YOUR ANSWER: Ways of delegating work may become habitual. For this reason it is a good idea to avoid the obvious; consider delegating in a different form or to different people.

You are correct.

When delegating work, it is very easy to overload a few people within the organization while ignoring others. This places an undue burden on some very competent persons and prevents the development and increase in capacity of others. We should delegate to develop people, we should not punish the more competent by giving him all the work, and, above all, we should not fall into the trap of doing work ourselves that can be or should be delegated to lower echelons of the organization.

You have completed the "To Whom Do You Delegate?" chapter. In the next chapter we will consider "Problems of Delegation." Please turn to section 158.

134

[from section 114]

YOUR ANSWER: The Governor was delegating correctly; he was delegating to the person who most needed the experience.

We do not know from the information given how much experience the analyst in Section C has.

It looks to us as if the delegation had become entangled in a mesh of improperly designated channels of communication. It would appear that the Governor, in the last analysis, actually delegated to subordinates of other people.

Please go back to section 114 and pick a better answer.

135

[from section 123]

YOUR ANSWER: The Chief Budget Analyst should recommend Alvin Linden because some jobs requiring thorough knowledge of a situation should be delegated to the lowest possible level at which capability of performing the task exists.

You are correct.

Neither the Governor nor the Chief Budget Analyst could avoid taking responsibility for the testimony that was made concerning the project. Nevertheless, the Grade III budget analyst had the information required to give the best testimony and was the person who should have been chosen for the job.

The Governor has his problems, but so do executives of other types of organizations. Let's see how small corporations are also faced with the question "To whom do we delegate?"

Ralph Hickman, general manager of the Atom Liner Guides Company, strode out into the manufacturing area of the company plant. He was obviously preoccupied and scarcely seemed to notice the persons who acknowledged his presence as he scurried past the various assembly stalls. He threw a perfunctory "Hello" to Floor Foreman Matty Gibb and, without pausing, continued on into Section 23 to talk to the chief of that section.

"We have a rush here," he said. "Stop what you are doing and go to work on this. Here are the specifications. The job will have to be completed by Friday night." Then Ralph turned on his heels and walked back to his office.

Ralph Hickman had bypassed his floor foreman, Matty Gibb, to delegate directly to the chief of Assembly Section 23. This made Gibb angry. Section 23 was already overloaded. He would much rather have had Section 19 do the job.

What would be good advice to give Ralph Hickman in *this* situation?

When you delegate, delegate to your immediate subordinate, not to your subordinate's subordinate. **section 128**

Delegate to the person who knows the job best. **section 144**

Do not always delegate to the person who customarily does the job; do the unusual. **section 155**

136
[from section 127]

YOUR ANSWER: The Governor was delegating to a person other than an immediate subordinate.

This is not entirely correct.

The Governor had learned his lesson. In this case, he wanted to talk directly with the person who would be doing the work, but he also wanted to have present those in the chain of command who would be affected. He was *not* asking the employee who would do the work to bypass his own superiors.

Please return to section 127 and make another choice.

137
[from section 116]

YOUR ANSWER: Delegate, or encourage delegation, to the person who is at the lowest organizational level at which performance capability exists.

You are correct.

This is one of the most important principles to keep in mind when considering to whom you should delegate. Always delegate —or encourage your subordinates to delegate—to the lowest organizational level at which there is a person who has the capability of performing the task effectively.

If you had taken the other choice, which indicated you should delegate to the person who has high status and authority, we would have told you you were wrong because there is no need to use such means to accomplish the work.

You are now ready for the Test Sequences. Please go on to section 138.

138
[from section 137]

TEST

Question No. 1.

It is said that the manager should delegate tasks to the lowest level of the organization at which capability to perform the task exists. It is also said that the manager should delegate only to persons who are his immediate subordinates. This would indicate:

Management theory is inconsistent. A manager might have a difficult time doing both. **section 119**

Managers must choose between one theory or the other. **section 130**

Perhaps both theories are wrong in the real world in which a manager must operate. **section 146**

If a manager thinks a subordinate of his subordinate can do the job he should say so, but he should delegate the job to his own immediate subordinate only. **section 151**

139
[from section 145]

YOUR ANSWER: The Budget Chief was delegating to weakness.

The information given does not state that Section D was weak, and we have no evidence to the effect that weakness existed. We think there is a better reason for the delegation: Section C was quite overloaded at the time and there seemed to be more available working time in Section D.

Please go back to section 145 and make another choice.

140
[from section 151]

YOUR ANSWER: It certainly makes sense under some circumstances to delegate a task to a person whose ability you wish to test, even though more capable employees are available for the task.

We agree.

While there are situations in which one should delegate to the person who knows the job best, there are other times at which it is advisable to test the capabilities of subordinates. There are many occasions when we have to measure long-term benefits against short-term gains. This would seem to be the case in this instance.

Question No. 3.

Ways of delegating work may become habitual. For this reason it is a good idea to:

Do the job yourself until you feel you know it; then delegate. **section 122**

Avoid the obvious; consider delegating in a different form or to different people. **section 133**

Delegate to the most competent person. **section 149**

Avoid delegating as a means of developing people. **section 154**

141
[from section 128]

YOUR ANSWER: A manager should always delegate to his immediate subordinate and should avoid the obvious. He should consider other persons than the one to whom it has become habitual to delegate.

You are correct.

We can gain a great deal by spreading the jobs to be done among a number of different persons. This has the advantage of bringing new points of view to bear upon situations, developing new skills, and preventing the overloading of the person who is particularly adept at a certain kind of job. This is not to say that competence should not be recognized. But when there is a choice, avoid the obvious.

It is permissible to discuss delegated tasks with others besides the person to whom you delegate. You delegate to your immediate subordinate; but you may discuss the delegation with many people, in order to give those who are associated with the project or task the information they need, or to obtain information that you as a manager need.

General Manager Ralph Hickman decided to form a task force to study possible reorganization of the Atom Liner Guides Company. In choosing the man to head the task force, he wavered between two of his four immediate subordinates: Al Middlestatt, in sales, had the most experience, but Floor Foreman Matty Gibb was scheduled to have more free time in the immediate future.

Hickman considered some rules of delegation he had learned:

1. One should delegate only to immediate subordinates.
2. One should avoid the obvious.
3. _____

86

Which of the following dicta is correct and belongs in the blank above?

One should delegate to persons with the most unused time. **section 121**

One should delegate to persons with the most experience. **section 152**

142
[from section 121]

YOUR ANSWER: One should:

1. Delegate only to immediate subordinates.
2. Avoid the obvious.
3. Delegate to the person having the most time.
4. Delegate to the person who has seniority.

This is not correct.

Frequently the seniority system takes over and forces management to assign persons not fitted to do the job to undertake the task. When management has a choice, it should delegate to the person with seniority only when there are other good reasons for so doing or when reasons are equal. In addition to the three reasons for choosing a particular person to whom to delegate, there is rationale for assigning tasks on the basis of providing new and profitable experiences for an employee.

Please go back to section 121 and make another choice.

143
[from section 117]

YOUR ANSWER: The Chief Budget Analyst was delegating to the lowest level of responsibility.

We have no evidence that this is the case.

He was really avoiding the obvious and giving others the opportunity to show what they could do with difficult problems. He was avoiding habitual thinking. Please go back to section 117 and make another choice.

144

[from section 135]

YOUR ANSWER: Good advice to Ralph Hickman, who had ignored the floor foreman and gone directly to the section head, would be: Delegate to the person who knows the job best.

This is not the correct answer.

Ralph Hickman bypassed his own immediate subordinate and gave work directly to a subordinate of his subordinate. This is in violation of the best practices of delegation. Remember that a good approach is to delegate only to one's immediate subordinate. We have had two or three illustrations in which not observing this rule led to organizational difficulty.

Please go back to section 135 and make another choice.

145

[from section 127]

YOUR ANSWER: The Governor was delegating to an immediate subordinate, but communicating directly with the one who would do the work.

You are correct.

This brings us a delicate but important concept in delegation. If instructions are to be understood clearly, it is frequently necessary to bring the person who is going to do the job face to face with the person who makes the initial assignment. Each time an assignment is relayed from one person to another through the chain of command, there is a chance for distortion and misunderstanding. When the job is of sufficient significance, and when understanding might involve complex communications, it is advisable to bring together the person who will do the job and the person who makes the initial assignment. It is possible to avoid bypassing the chain of command by having those persons present who are "in the middle" of the discussion. Those "in the middle" should know what goes on; action taken by subordinates should be reviewed by them.

Here is another problem. Ordinarily, the Chief Budget Analyst would assign a person from Section C to work on social welfare problems. He was aware, however, that unit work loads varied and that there was a necessity to maintain a balance. This time, how-

ever, he felt that Section D had more time to work on the assignment than did Section C, and he gave the job to Section D. In this
case, the Budget Chief was:

Delegating to the unit that had the greatest available free time.
section 117

Delegating to weakness. **section 139**

Delegating to the lowest level at which capability existed to do the
job. **section 156**

146
[from section 138]

YOUR ANSWER: It is said that the manager should delegate tasks
to the lowest level of competence, and that he should delegate only
to persons who are his immediate subordinates. Perhaps both theories are wrong in the real world in which a manager must operate.

It is obvious that no principle applies universally in a job as complex as that of management. Nevertheless, we can say that it is generally true that a manager should delegate only to his immediate
subordinate and that it is generally true that tasks should be delegated to the lowest level of the organization at which capability to
perform the tasks exists.

These concepts are not in conflict. Each manager has the obligation of passing the delegation downward as far as capability to
perform the tasks exists.

Please go back to section 138 and pick again.

147
[from section 151]

YOUR ANSWER: Theoretically, delegating a task to a person
whose ability you wish to test when others more capable are available for the assignment, sounds good; but in practice, the big job is
to get the "show on the road." Why waste time?

We think there is a better answer.
The temptation exists to get the "show on the road." The temp-

tation is to feel that delegating to a person who is not thoroughly conversant with the task is a waste of time.

Under some circumstances, one certainly would want immediate results. It is necessary, however, for the manager to take a long-term view of many of his activities and to sacrifice short-term gains for long-term benefits. For this reason it is often a good idea to test the readiness of subordinates to move ahead and to try out their capabilities to perform certain jobs.

Please return to section 151 and make another choice.

148
[from section 115]

YOUR ANSWER: To test the abilities of subordinates, one should delegate only those tasks he knows how to do.

Under many circumstances, it is a good idea to delegate to a person when you wish to test his abilities. The case we are considering is a case where Joe, the Grade III budget analyst, apparently had all the capabilities that would be required of a senior analyst. He was, however, untried. There was no way of knowing how he would react under the stress of a difficult situation until he actually was tested. The only way to test him was to delegate and actually see how he performed.

Please return to section 115 and make another choice.

149
[from section 140]

YOUR ANSWER: Ways of delegating work may become habitual. For this reason it is a good idea to delegate to the most competent person.

As reasonable as this may sound, it is not the expected answer.

The most competent person is generally overloaded, but still capable of taking on more work. This does not mean that the circumstances that cause this are desirable. It might be that other people would become more competent if the work were delegated to them and if they had the responsibility for carrying it out. It is easy to become dependent on a few people and adopt habitual patterns of delegating. For this reason, it is a very good idea to vary our approach to delegation, both as to the form in which the delegation is given and as to the persons to whom specific jobs are delegated.

Please go back to section 140 and make another selection.

150
[from section 123]

YOUR ANSWER: The Chief Budget Analyst should recommend Alvin Linden because you should never stick your own neck out unless you have to.

A manager is forever sticking his neck out. The person who is afraid to expose himself gets little done. An effective manager is an active person who is capable of taking necessary risks.

In this case, passing the buck to a lower echelon would not help the Chief Budget Analyst. If the Grade III who happened to be very familiar with the project did not do a good job with the legislative committee, the Chief Budget Analyst and the Governor would both suffer just as surely as if they had given the testimony themselves. Avoiding risks is never a good reason for delegation. As a matter of fact, delegation generally increases risk. The reason for increasing risk is to be able to extend oneself and get more done through people.

Please go back to section 123 and make another choice.

151
[from section 138]

YOUR ANSWER: It is said that the manager should delegate tasks to the lowest level of competence and that he should delegate only to persons who are his immediate subordinates. If a manager thinks a subordinate of his subordinate can do the job, he should say so, but he should delegate the job to his own immediate subordinate only.

You are correct.

The theories stated in the premise are not in conflict if viewed in the manner in which you have answered. A manager may delegate to his subordinate only, but he expects his subordinate to delegate downward to capable persons within the organization.

Question No. 2.

It is sometimes desirable to delegate a task to a person whose ability you wish to test, even though more capable employees are available for the assignment.

I disagree. **section 131**

This certainly makes sense under some circumstances. **section 140**

Theoretically this sounds good; but in practice the big job is to get the "show on the road." Why waste time? **section 147**

Why sometimes? It is always desirable to develop talent in your organization. This is a good way to do it. **section 157**

152
[from section 141]

YOUR ANSWER: Some good rules of delegation are:

1. One should delegate only to immediate subordinates.
2. One should avoid the obvious.
3. One should delegate to persons with the most experience.

Persons known to be most experienced should be considered when delegation occurs. However, they are not always in the best position to judge whether or not they should be given the new job. The boss should also consider persons in the establishment who seem to have less to do than others, persons with the most unused time.

Please go back to section 141 and make another choice.

YOUR ANSWER: The manager should delegate to the person who most needs to develop his skills.

This is not the "better" answer.

It sometimes helps to delegate to a person in order to assist him in developing his skills, but this does not mean that it is good policy or even, in many cases, a good risk to delegate to the person who most needs to develop his skills. It may be that people should develop their skills gradually. Jobs should be delegated as people develop the ability to handle them successfully. From time to time it is a good idea to delegate to find out if persons are capable of higher-level work. This is a far cry from delegating to the person who most needs to develop his skills.

Please go back to section 129 and make another choice.

YOUR ANSWER: Ways of delegating work may become habitual. For this reason it is a good idea to avoid delegating as a means of developing people.

This is not correct.

One answer to the question "To whom should I delegate?" is "I should delegate to a person who will develop because I give him this job to do." In other words, one of the best ways of developing subordinates is to delegate to them. Nevertheless, development is not the *only* reason for delegating responsibility and authority. There are many reasons.

In answering this question, we were considering the circumstance in which methods of delegation become habitual. It seems to us that it is a very good idea to avoid delegating in the same old way to the same old person day after day. It is a good idea to consider delegating in different forms and to different people.

Please go back to section 140 and make another selection.

155

[from section 135]

YOUR ANSWER: Good advice to Ralph Hickman, who ignored his floor foreman and went directly to the chief of Assembly Section 23, would be: Do not always delegate to the person who customarily does the job; do the unusual.

It is a good idea to avoid the usual and to discover persons who have not previously handled the work. But in this case, we are discussing a different matter. We are talking about a general manager who ignored the floor foreman and went directly to the chief of an assembly section. The general manager did not know the full situation on the floor. The floor foreman did; the floor foreman was the immediate subordinate of the general manager, and our rule is to delegate only to our own immediate subordinate.

Please go back to section 135 and make another choice.

156

[from section 145]

YOUR ANSWER: The Budget Chief was delegating to the lowest level at which capability existed to do the job.

This is not entirely correct.

Delegating to the lowest level at which capability exists is one of the principles of delegation. If this question were involved we would say the Chief Budget Analyst should certainly adhere to that principle. However, in this case, delegating to the lowest level is not the issue.

The Budget Chief was delegating to Section D because that section apparently had more free time than Section C.

Please go back to section 145 and make another choice.

YOUR ANSWER: It is sometimes desirable to delegate a task to a person whose ability you wish to test, even though more capable employees are available for the assignment. I say: Why sometimes? It is *always* desirable to develop the talent in your organization. This is a good way to do it.

There is a better answer.

There are probably many situations in which it is desirable to delegate to the person who is the expert—who can "get the show on the road" without wasting time. We realize that the temptation is in this direction, rather than in taking the long-term view. Nevertheless, there is something to be said for both sides of the question. In general, we think that one of the factors that should be considered when delegating is delegating in order to test readiness of employees to move ahead. But this is only one of many criteria which should be applied.

Please go back to section 151 and make another choice.

Chapter 5

PROBLEMS OF DELEGATION

There is sometimes a reluctance to delegate or to be delegated to. The executive is sometimes reluctant to delegate for one or more of the following reasons:

He suffers from feelings of personal insecurity.

He feels he is more competent than his subordinates.

He is afraid of not knowing the answers.

He is afraid of developing his own competition.

He feels unable to define objectives with sufficient clarity.

Subordinates, on their part, are sometimes reluctant to accept delegation for one or more of the following reasons:

They don't understand the task.

It's easier to ask the boss than it is to figure it out.

They have a high rate of dependency.

They fear criticism.

They lack belief in their own competence.

They are already overburdened with work.

They lack identification with the enterprise.

We are, by now, quite familiar with the Green Front Grocery chain. Let's once again use this company to illustrate problems of delegation.

Sam finally assumed the title of president of the chain. Green Front had become a sizable organization. In large measure, Sam had built the business himself. He knew many of the details of the operation. As the business grew, he could not personally keep up with everything. He had to rely on staff and subordinates for information.

The store managers respected Sam's alertness and ability to ask the right questions. For example, he would ask Charles Shultz in Green Front Grocery No. 3, "How many sides of beef did your meat section sell on Thursday?" or "How are those new cash registers working? Do they save time?" or "Are deliveries of fresh produce being made when they are due?" or "How many two-month-old cans of solid-pack tomatoes do you have on the shelf?"

With a boss like Sam, store managers had to keep very close track of what was going on in the store; they were reluctant to delegate.

What caused this reluctance to delegate?

Fear that delegation might make working employees look better than the store manager. **section 164**

Fear of not knowing the answers. **section 171**

159
[from section 168]

YOUR ANSWER: Harry Quint did not feel responsible for the mistake made by his subordinate.

Harry Quint *should* feel responsible for the mistake, because he cannot delegate his own overall responsibility.

We would rather believe that in this instance Harry was giving his subordinate a chance to learn from his own mistakes. He was not glossing over the fact that a mistake had been made. He was saying that, in general, he had confidence in the judgment of the man to whom he had delegated.

Please go back to section 168 and make another choice.

160
[from section 167]

YOUR ANSWER: Fear of competition from developing subordinates might cause some managers to avoid delegation.

You are correct.

Frequently managers are fearful that their employees will become more competent than themselves. This is a major block to delegation in many organizational settings.

Sometimes managers do not delegate because they themselves can do the job better (even though, in the long run, this does not make for greater efficiency); sometimes their motive is a desire to protect the employee, although this is less frequent.

Question No. 3.

Professional persons placed in managerial positions often have difficulty in delegating because:

They have an insufficient amount of managerial duties assigned to them. **section 169**

Other professionals do not need managing. **section 175**

They have a fear of not knowing the answer. **section 187**

They can do the assigned task better than can the subordinates.
section 196

161
[from section 172]

YOUR ANSWER: Kern did not believe in his own competence.

We do not have enough evidence to go on.
Kern did arrange vegetables under the tutelage of George Gable. Kern probably would tell his wife or his friends that he knew how to buy tomatoes, but with George Gable, an experienced produce man, as his boss, it was easier simply to ask the boss and avoid making the decision himself.
We think that it would be worthwhile to check another answer. Please return to section 172 and make another choice.

162
[from section 201]

YOUR ANSWER: Marian did not identify with the company.

This is not the answer.
The PBX board was busy; Marian did typing when the phone did not keep her busy; but checking invoices and bills, which required some special attention to detail, was too much for her to handle. She began getting sick and became an absentee problem.
We are not absolutely sure of the facts, but it seems as if she may

have been overworked. The invoices and bills of lading might have been the "straw that broke the camel's back."

Please return to section 201 and try another answer.

163
[from section 195]

YOUR ANSWER: One problem in delegation is a fear most of us have of looking bad to the boss.

You are correct.

Most of us do have a desire to look good to the boss. This often causes us to "do it ourselves" when we should have the work done through others.

Let us continue to examine problems connected with delegation.

George Gable had managed the produce section before becoming store manager. He "knew his onions," as the saying goes. Although Jay Kern, his produce man, seemed eager to please, George found himself helping with the vegetables every day. This, he said, was because he could get things done better and faster himself.

Did George Gable's attitude and actions contribute to delegation or interfere with it?

They contributed to delegation. **section 179**

They interfered with delegation. **section 188**

164
[from section 158]

YOUR ANSWER: Fear that delegation might make working employees look better than the store manager made some managers reluctant to delegate.

Perhaps. Let's talk about it.

Some persons are so constituted that they believe they must downgrade the other person in order to gain merit for themselves.

But most people are not like this. With a question-asking boss like Sam, a manager might keep very close track of all of the minute details in the store, but we think it would be generally because of a fear of not being able to give Sam the answers rather than a fear that the other employees would look too good. There is some justification for your point of view. Nevertheless, we would like you to go back to section 158 and make another choice.

165

[from section 189]

YOUR ANSWER: Apathy causes the employee to resist accepting delegation.

No, this is not the correct answer.

In our times, we have seen the effect of apathy upon work. A number of employees are apathetic toward work, and there are many reasons for this. One cause of apathy is the lack of identification with the enterprise.

However, we think that in this case a greater problem is the employee's unwillingness to be held accountable for results.

Please return to section 189 and make another choice.

166

[from section 178]

YOUR ANSWER: Resentment at being asked to do a job with lower status than that of secretary might have been responsible for Patricia's reluctance to accept the delegation.

While this might be true, we think there is a better reason.

A PBX board can be quite formidable to the untutored and untrained. Patricia did not know how to run the board. In other words, she had been asked to do a job she did not know how to do. It might be that her reluctance was due to the feeling that she was not capable of doing the job she was asked to do.

At any rate, we hope that you will make another choice. Please go back to section 178.

YOUR ANSWER: To delegate, a manager must have a feeling of security.

You are correct.

Managers frequently do not delegate when they should because they feel it is not safe: They feel that the jobs will not be executed according to a quality that will make them look good; they feel that somehow or other their status, their reputation, or their job is threatened.

Managers also frequently do not delegate because they have risen to management positions from professional and technical backgrounds and it is difficult for a person to put his specialty in the background and to spend his energies on management functions when his major interest is in his professional field.

TEST

Question No. 2.

Some managers hold on to vital information and key duties which they should delegate to employees. What might this be due to?

Fear of competition from developing employees. **section 160**

An effort to keep down unrest in the organization. **section 174**

A desire for greater efficiency. **section 180**

A desire to protect the employee. **section 200**

168

[from section 203]

YOUR ANSWER: He would have been reacting from his anxiety or fear of the boss.

You are correct.

Sam had found a deviation from expected performance and had held Harry Quint, the store manager, responsible for the deviation. Harry might have taken corrective action by telling Ambrose to check with him before buying anything. This would have been a poor corrective action; Harry should concern himself with improving Ambrose's buying ability, rather than with trying to control the past. In any case, he would have been reacting from anxiety or fear of his boss if he had retracted his delegation.

On the other hand, Harry might have reacted by saying, "The boss was hopping mad about the sweet corn, but it seemed like a good deal at the time. Maybe we've learned something worthwhile. Your judgment has been good in the past and seems to me to be getting better. Keep on calling the shots as you see them."

What would this approach indicate about Harry's managerial philosophy?

Harry Quint did not feel responsible for the mistake made by his subordinate. **section 159**

Harry Quint was willing to let a subordinate learn from his mistakes. **section 181**

169

[from section 160]

YOUR ANSWER: Professional persons placed in managerial positions often have difficulty in delegating because they have an insufficient amount of managerial duties assigned to them.

Based on the information contained in the question, we would be assuming a great deal if we assumed that managers have an insufficient amount of managerial duties assigned to them. Knowing what we know about many management jobs, we have some doubts that most managers have too little managing to do. We think that the answer can be found in a different area. We think that professional persons are highly identified with their profession. In general they believe themselves to be highly competent persons, and frequently they believe they can do the jobs better than the persons they would be forced to delegate the duties to.

Please go back to section 160 and make another choice.

170

[from section 196]

YOUR ANSWER: An employee who likes to accept delegation is capable of seeking answers from the boss.

An employee who likes to accept delegation might be capable of seeking answers from the boss, but this is so loosely connected that we think a better answer is called for. The employee who is able to accept delegation is one who has a sense of security, a reliance in his own competence, and ability to act on his own.

Please go back to section 196 and make another choice.

171

[from section 158]

YOUR ANSWER: Fear of not knowing the answers made some managers reluctant to delegate.

Right.

When top managers ask questions concerning the details of operations and indicate that they want the answers, it is only natural for intermediary managers to submerge themselves in the kind of detail they think the boss will want to know.

Suppose that, when Sam asked about the sale of beef, Charles Shultz replied, "I haven't talked to my meat manager, but I assume he would have let me know if anything unusual had occurred. I'll check with him and call you right back."

And suppose further that Sam then said, "This is the kind of thing I expect my managers to know. Why do you have to ask the meat manager?"

Then, based on these suppositions, what would result?

Charles probably would spend a great deal of time on detail, and neglect other parts of his job. **section 177**

Charles would laugh it off; bosses being bosses, Sam would just have to be tolerated. **section 186**

172

[from section 199]

YOUR ANSWER: The store manager did not understand what he was supposed to do.

That is correct.

He understood only that he was supposed to make a profit. He did not understand that his job also included building up the business by courteous treatment to customers, by cleanliness, and by service.

It might also have been that he did not feel a personal responsibility for the interests of the company. An employee who identifies with the company has the feeling that the well-being of the company is also his well-being.

Employees have other problems related to delegation. These are concerned with the need for reassurance and support, and they also involve ignorance, indifference, and laziness. Let's get specific.

At Green Front Store No. 1, Jay Kern in produce would come constantly to George Gable and say, "How shall I arrange the citrus fruit?" or "How many tomatoes do you think we need?"

What seems to be the problem here?

Kern did not believe in his own competence. **section 161**

It was easier for Kern to ask the boss than to figure things out for himself. **section 189**

YOUR ANSWER: Managers should be made of sterner stuff and should not crumple psychologically before the boss.

This is not the lesson on interpersonal relations, but it is true that almost all of us are profoundly influenced by the attitudes and actions of our bosses. We agree that managers should be made of sterner stuff. We may not actually "crumple," but we do like to look as good as possible.

There is, however, a better answer. Please return to section 195 and make another choice.

YOUR ANSWER: An effort to keep down unrest in the organization might cause some managers to avoid delegation.

There probably are occasions when delegation causes unrest and discomfort in an organization. On the other hand, there are many instances in which delegation has enlivened an organization and put it back on its feet. Since delegation is necessary, a manager should learn to delegate in a manner that does not cause undue unrest. We think, however, this is a minor danger.

A more common reason for not delegating is the growth and development a manager sees and fears in his subordinates.

Please return to section 167 and make another choice.

YOUR ANSWER: Professional persons placed in managerial positions often have difficulty in delegating because other professionals do not need managing.

We would like to argue this point with you a bit.

We have heard that professionals do not need to be managed. We have heard that creative persons cannot be curtailed with mundane procedures. To a certain extent, perhaps, both of these are true. But, the more professional or technical the work, the more difficult become the interrelationships between people in a work unit, and the more need there is to coordinate the efforts of all involved.

In the question you are attempting to answer, there is a different area worthy of examination. Executives frequently do not assign tasks to subordinates because they believe themselves to be able to do these jobs better and faster than the persons to whom they might assign them. Please go back to section 160 and make another choice.

176

[from section 196]

YOUR ANSWER: An employee who likes to accept delegation is a person who has achieved a degree of independence.

You are correct.

In general, the person who has achieved independence is capable of accepting delegation. We would expect him to be confident of his own abilities and free from much of the fear of criticism that a more dependent person would have.

GENERAL PRINCIPLES

The responsibility that is to be delegated and the authority that accompanies it should be clearly defined, preferably in writing.

Authority should be delegated that is commensurate with the responsibility to be discharged.

A person should be accountable only to the one person who delegates authority and responsibility to him.

The degree of delegation should be proportional to the availability of effective controls.

Congratulations. You have now completed the course on delegation. From it, you should have gathered that Sam could never have expanded his business without extending himself by vesting in others the right to act in his behalf. You cannot extend yourself unless you learn to get work done through others—unless you learn to delegate.

Delegation is the measure of a manager.

177

[from section 171]

YOUR ANSWER: Charles would probably spend a great deal of time on detail, and neglect other parts of his job.

You are correct.

If you expect your subordinates to be up-to-date on minutiae, you will be making it difficult for them to delegate to people who work for them.

By the same token, if your own superior expects you to know this kind of detail, delegation will be difficult for you. (If you do find yourself in this unfortunate situation, perhaps you can talk it over with your boss and reach an understanding.)

But what if it had not happened that way? Suppose Sam had, instead, said to Charles, "O.K., call me back. I have a special reason for needing the information. Just find out from your meat manager."

What, then, is the probable result?

Charles might still feel that he must know more detail. **section 184**

Charles might feel less necessity to burden himself with detail.
section 195

178

[from section 189]

YOUR ANSWER: Fear of criticism causes the employee to resist accepting delegation.

Of course.

Employees need to look good to their boss, to their fellow employees, and to themselves. When assigned a new job, there is a possibility of failure. Unwillingness to attack the unknown frequently arises from fear of ridicule or sanction from fellow employees or authority figures. A major problem of employees in accepting delegation is fear of criticism.

And there are, of course, other problems.

At Sam's downtown office, the headquarters of Green Front Groceries, there was a PBX board with direct lines to a number of store installations. Patricia, Sam's secretary, was asked to take over one day when the regular PBX operator was sick. She cried, but finally agreed to do it.

What might have been responsible for her reluctance to accept this delegation?

Resentment at being asked to do a job with lower status than that of secretary. **section 166**

Lack of belief in her own competence to do the job. **section 201**

179
[*from section 163*]

YOUR ANSWER: George Gable's attitude and actions contributed to delegation.

It doesn't seem reasonable that they should.

George Gable was an experienced produce man. He was able to work effectively in the produce department, and the chances are he could work faster and better than his subordinate, Jay Kern. But Jay Kern could not be expected to learn or develop his proficiency if George did all the work. Therefore, George's actions must have interfered with delegation—not contributed.

Please return to section 163 and make another choice.

180
[*from section 167*]

YOUR ANSWER: A desire for greater efficiency might cause some managers to avoid delegation.

This is not the correct answer, although there is some truth in the answer you have chosen.

Some managers "do it themselves" because they are more adept than their subordinates at completing the tasks. Of course, their subordinates will never learn unless they are given the opportunity. So, in the end, even though the desire might be for greater efficiency, avoiding delegation is not the way to work things out.

Please return to section 167 and make another choice.

181

[from section 168]

YOUR ANSWER: Harry Quint was willing to let a subordinate learn from his mistakes.

This is correct.

Successful delegation depends, in part, upon the boss's willingness to let subordinates learn from their mistakes. This does not mean glossing over mistakes or hiding the consequences of mistakes from the person who made them. It *does* mean demonstrating confidence in the employee's ability to do the job and learn as he goes along.

Now for another problem. In a previous lesson we examined the case of the store manager who was so intent on immediate profits that he lost out in the long run. As a consequence of his shortsightedness, the competitor gained customers while Green Front merely held at the same level. Sam believed in making money, but he knew it was also important to increase customers and expand the business. The manager, however, did not grasp the need to look for total expected results, but concentrated on short-term profits.

What would you cite here as the cause of the trouble?

Poor judgment on the part of the store manager. **section 193**

Poor definition and understanding of objectives. **section 199**

182

[from section 201]

YOUR ANSWER: Marian was already overburdened with work.

You are correct.

The PBX board was busy. Marian had typing duties that kept her busy when the phone was not ringing. The addition of the bills of lading and invoices put a demand on her she did not feel able to meet.

Let us examine one more problem.

Lillie Bishop was a checker at Green Front Grocery No. 4, where Wilbur Potts was manager. She was accurate and fast; she was prompt, courteous, and a hard worker; but she would not work one minute after quitting time and refused to take on additional responsibility, even though Wilbur tried to explain that it would be to her advantage to do so. Her answer was that she was only working for the money.

It was evident why Lillie would not accept more delegation.
What was the reason?

Lillie did not identify herself with the company. **section 197**

Lillie had no interest in her work. **section 204**

183
[*from section 199*]

YOUR ANSWER: The manager was not looking out for the well-being of the company.

There might be something to this, but it is not the expected answer.

We think that the Green Front store manager who pushed for quick profits at the expense of long-term customer relations really did not understand what he was supposed to do.

Now, it might also be true that he was not looking out for the well-being of the company. It might be that he was more concerned with making a profit himself than with furthering the interests of the company.

Please return to section 199 and make another choice.

184
[*from section 177*]

YOUR ANSWER: Charles might still feel that he must know more detail.

It is possible, but . . .
By answering in this vein, Sam would have made it easier for

Charles to delegate to his meat manager. It would have become acceptable to ask the meat manager about detail. In other words, Charles was not expected to carry the detail in his own mind.

Please go back to section 177 and make another choice.

185

[from section 198]

YOUR ANSWER: Managers need to feel dependent and are therefore reluctant to delegate.

This is not the correct answer.

One cause of tension and conflict within a manager is the feeling of dependence he sometimes gets when he must act in an independent way. Managers do not need to feel dependent; rather, managers must feel safe to delegate.

Please return to section 198 and make another choice.

186

[from section 171]

YOUR ANSWER: Charles would laugh it off; bosses being bosses, Sam would just have to be tolerated.

Laughing off the viewpoints of the boss can become an imprudent type of activity, one not always calculated to induce long tenure with an organization.

If Sam, as the head of the firm, demands detailed knowledge of minutiae from his subordinates, the chances are they will try to keep abreast of such minutiae in order to give it to him.

In delegating, one should permit subordinates to get away from unnecessary detail.

Please return to section 171 and make another choice.

187

[from section 160]

YOUR ANSWER: Professional persons placed in managerial positions often have difficulty in delegating because they have a fear of not knowing the answer.

In general, professional persons would have less fear of not knowing some of the answers than persons who are not so highly trained. In any case, we do not think this is the reason that professionals have difficulty in delegation.

We think that professionals are highly identified with their professions. They believe themselves to be competent in their professional field. Frequently they believe they can do the assigned tasks better than can subordinates to whom they might delegate. Besides, they often enjoy their professional work more than they enjoy their managerial work.

Please go back to section 160 and make another choice.

188

[from section 163]

YOUR ANSWER: George Gable's attitudes and actions interfered with delegation.

Of course.

It is quite possible that George could do the work in the produce department faster and better than Jay Kern. Nevertheless, Jay could not be expected to develop his proficiency or learn how to do things for himself if George always took over. One of the major reasons for failure in delegation is the fact that the supervisor can in many cases do things better and faster himself and hence continue to do the work. But the supervisor cannot do *everything* in the organization himself. When he continues to do his old job, the true management functions which he should be performing are usually neglected.

Charles Shultz felt sufficiently secure to stay out of the details in the management of his store. He began to notice, however, that Sam was bypassing him and asking more and more specific questions of the meat manager and the produce manager. While Sam didn't seem to mind, Charles began to worry.

What do you think it was that caused Charles to worry?

112

Fear of not knowing the answers. **section 194**

Fear of competition. **section 203**

189
[from section 172]

YOUR ANSWER: It was easier for Kern to ask the boss than to figure things out for himself.

You are correct.

And this is one of the major problems in delegation. Frequently the boss is very competent in the field. It is quite easy to go to the boss and say, "How would you do this?" and very easy for the boss to answer. It is also easy to bolster a picture of inadequacy that an employee has of himself if the boss is always willing to take responsibility for him.

One of the problems in delegation from the standpoint of the employee is the feeling that he is incapable of doing the job that is delegated to him.

Some employees are not capable of making decisions and carrying out assigned duties.

When an employee needs help in order to make decisions and carry out duties, he can be said to be dependent. Some employees have been brought up to feel dependent upon authority. This acts as a real barrier to delegation. Such employees must learn to act on their own if they are to become truly effective. They will only do so if they are allowed to build up confidence in themselves by being given jobs that they can complete successfully. Many dependent employees do well if they are given instructions in detail, but are inept when expected to use initiative.

Employees are often afraid to undertake new tasks or accept delegation because they fear the boss or their fellow employees might ridicule them.

Which of the choices below applies in such a case?

Apathy causes the employee to resist accepting delegation. **section 165**

Fear of criticism causes the employee to resist accepting delegation. **section 178**

190

[from section 198]

YOUR ANSWER: The executive identifies highly with the enterprise and is therefore reluctant to delegate.

This is not the correct answer.

It is probably true that managers tend to identify very closely with their organization or enterprise. This has many virtues, although it also causes some personal problems. Nevertheless, this is not the answer to the question we were asking.

Identification does not interfere with delegation. Rather, the manager fails to delegate because of a fear that he in some way will be the loser by the delegation.

Please return to section 198 and make another choice.

191

[from section 196]

YOUR ANSWER: An employee who likes to accept delegation is prone to fear criticism.

No, this is not correct.

An employee who is prone to fear criticism is less likely to accept delegation than one who feels that he has competence and that he is not likely to be criticized for what he does.

Please return to section 196 and make another choice.

192

[from section 203]

YOUR ANSWER: He would have been justified; he was checking closely into the activities of a man who makes mistakes.

When tasks are delegated, management controls should be set up; these controls should enable management to set standards, check to see that standards are being observed, and take corrective action if standards are not being observed.

However, we do not think that Harry Quint would be justified in checking so closely into the activities of the man who made this

114

mistake as to inhibit his future activities and value to the company. There are other corrective actions that would be more effective.

Please go back to section 203 and make another choice.

193
[from section 181]

YOUR ANSWER: Poor judgment on the part of the store manager was the cause of the trouble.

We do not know whether this was true or not.

In the case in question, the manager was out to make a quick profit for the store; he was willing to do so at the expense of long-term future relations with customers and at the expense of a proper share of future business in the neighborhood.

We do not think this was due to poor judgment. Rather, we think it was due to a lack of understanding of his job and of the purpose of the company.

Please return to section 181 and make another choice.

194
[from section 188]

YOUR ANSWER: Fear of not knowing the answers caused Charles to worry.

Charles had given up trying to answer Sam's questions directly. Sam wanted detailed answers faster and began to ask the subordinates directly. Charles may then have felt left out or bypassed; perhaps he began to fear that his subordinates would look better than he would himself.

Please return to section 188 and make another choice.

195

[from section 177]

YOUR ANSWER: Charles might feel less necessity to burden himself with detail.

You are correct.

As a manager, you should make it possible for your subordinates to delegate work to others. This does not mean that you should be cut off from information; but you should be content to receive information from those persons at a lower level who are capable of answering questions in detail.

What can we deduce from the impact of Sam's actions upon Charles Shultz, and from the difference in Shultz's response to the different approaches?

One problem in delegation is a fear most of us have of looking bad to the boss. **section 163**

Managers should be made of sterner stuff and should not crumple psychologically before the boss. **section 173**

196

[from section 160]

YOUR ANSWER: Professional persons placed in managerial positions often have difficulty in delegating because they can do the assigned task better than can the subordinates.

You are correct.

Persons assigned to management positions from professional fields have difficulty at first in delegating elements of their work. They are highly skilled in their profession. Most of them have been competent practitioners, and they have practiced a long time. They feel themselves to be effective, and they enjoy the professional job. Often, therefore, they believe they can do work that normally would be assigned to subordinates better than can the subordinates to whom they might assign it.

Question No. 4.

An employee who likes to accept delegation is:

Capable of seeking answers from the boss. **section 170**

A person who has achieved a degree of independence. **section 176**

Prone to fear criticism. **section 191**

One who is fairly dependent. **section 202**

197
[from section 182]

YOUR ANSWER: Lillie would not accept more delegation because she did not identify herself with the company.

You are correct.

An employee who identifies with the company is interested in the well-being of that organization, and not simply in what the organization can give him. He feels himself to be a part of the organization, and the organization is important to him.

Lillie was a good hard worker, interested in performing well so that she could get her paycheck at the end of the week. But she had no interest in the ultimate well-being of the company.

While this is a special problem with women workers, it is also a general problem with all workers in almost any organization. The manager who seeks to delegate should be aware that delegation is sometimes a problem because employees have not identified with the organization for which they work.

You have now completed the lesson. Please go on to section 198 and try a short test.

TEST

Question No. 1.

Managers frequently do not delegate even when they know they should. What is responsible for this reluctance?

To delegate, a manager must have a feeling of security.　section 167

Managers need to feel dependent.　section 185

The executive identifies highly with the enterprise.　section 190

The manager has little background in technical fields.　section 205

199
[*from section 181*]

YOUR ANSWER: Poor definition and understanding of objectives were the causes of the trouble.

You are correct.

And this highlights a major problem that a manager has in delegating: It is the problem of properly defining objectives and goals of the organization so that they are understood and accepted by subordinates.

We have been examining problems that the boss has in delegating. Now let's examine the other side of the coin.

We are going to consider some delegation problems from the point of view of the subordinate.

Let's consider the case of a shortsighted manager, who overlooked courtesy, cleanliness, and service for the sake of immediate profits. What caused this difficulty?

The manager did not understand what he was supposed to do.

section 172

The manager was not looking out for the well-being of the company.　section 183

YOUR ANSWER: A desire to protect the employee might cause some managers to avoid delegation.

Some managers protect employees by not delegating, but we doubt if this is a major reason for failure to delegate. We think there is a better answer, which has to do with the fear some managers have of employees who come along too fast and offer too much competition.

Please return to section 167 and make another choice.

YOUR ANSWER: Lack of belief in her own competence to do the job might have been responsible for Patricia's reluctance to accept the delegation.

People are fearful of undertaking tasks that they feel unable to do. A problem to the employee in receiving delegation is his lack of belief in his own competence to do the delegated job.

Sometimes, though, the unwillingness to accept new delegations does not stem from lack of self-confidence, but from too much work that has already been assigned.

Marian was the regular PBX board operator. In addition to watching the phone, Marian also did some typing. Sam felt it would be useful if Marian could also check invoices and bills of lading on special shipments. So he assigned her these duties. Shortly after they had been added, Marian began to be absent frequently. She told Sam she just didn't see how she could hold up under the added work.

What was Marian's delegation problem?

She did not identify with the company.   **section 162**

She was already overburdened with work.   **section 182**

202

[from section 196]

YOUR ANSWER: An employee who likes to accept delegation is one who is fairly dependent.

A dependent employee is one who is unwilling to move on his own. He does not have a high degree of initiative. He is prone to fear criticism. He likes to have the boss make decisions for him. Such a person is not amenable to assuming a high degree of delegation.

Please return to section 196 and make another choice.

203

[from section 188]

YOUR ANSWER: Fear of competition caused Charles to worry.

You are correct.

When communication bypasses a supervisor and takes place between the top boss and a subordinate, the supervisor is inclined to feel a little uneasy. One of the blocks to delegation is this fear that our subordinates will begin to demonstrate more competence than we do ourselves and will eventually, therefore, supersede us. Fear of competition, fear for our own position, and fear of criticism are very real factors acting toward the prevention of delegation.

Let's bring in still more problems.

Kenneth Ambrose, acting on his own as he had been taught to do, made an error in judgment and overbought on sweet corn for Green Front Store No. 5. Sam was hopping mad when he found out; he expressed his displeasure in no uncertain terms to manager Harry Quint.

There are several ways in which Harry could have reacted to this scolding. For one thing, he might have become angry with Ambrose and told him: "From now on, you check with me before you buy anything."

Suppose he had reacted in this way; would he have been justified, or merely reacting out of his anxiety?

He would have been reacting from his anxiety or fear of the boss.
section 168

He would have been justified; he was checking closely into the activities of a man who makes mistakes. **section 192**

204
[from section 182]

YOUR ANSWER: Lillie would not accept more delegation because she had no interest in her work.

This is not the correct answer.

The case sets forth the fact that Lillie was accurate and fast, prompt and courteous, and a hard worker. She did have an interest in her work—she was working for the money—but she wanted to quit when the hour of quitting arrived, and she did not particularly care about the prosperity of the organization. Please return to section 182 and make another choice.

205
[from section 198]

YOUR ANSWER: The manager has little background in technical fields and is therefore reluctant to delegate.

Quite the contrary. Managers frequently have extensive technical background in a portion of the activities they are called upon to supervise. A technical background sometimes gets in the way of good management because the manager would rather operate as a technician than as an executive.

In this question we were talking about a situation in which the manager does not feel right about delegating, because of expected consequences. Please return to section 198 and make another choice.

Index

This index has been designed both to help you review major subjects covered in this course and to make it easy for you to look up our comments on various special topics. The numbers given apply to sections, and in some cases, the numerical reference designates a section in which a topic-sequence begins.

Accountability:
  definition, 1
  example of, 5
Assignment of work:
  by function, 20
  by location, 8
Authority:
  definition, 1
  example of, 12, 31
  investment of, 23

Chain of command, 128, 145
Communication, 118, 128
Control systems, 33, 91, 96, 102
Coordination, 12

Defining objectives, 67, 181
Delegating to weakness, 117
Delegation:
  definition, 1
  importance of, 16
  problems of, 158

Fear factors, 189, 203
Financial negotiation, 41

Hot potatoes, 36

Learning from mistakes, 168
Levels of command, 114
Long-range planning, 41

Manager:
  specific duties of, 36
Measuring results, 80

Organization, 41
Overwork, 201

Personal identification with
  company goals, 182, 199, 201
Progress reports, 91

Responsibility:
  assigning, 101
  definition, 1
  example of, 16
  obligations of the manager, 31
Rewards and punishments, 65

Seniority, 129
Specialized skills, 65
Status, 53
Subordinates:
  appraising, 52
  developing, 40, 58, 132
  testing, 58, 123

Target dates, 101, 104
Test questions:
  Chapter 1, 11

Chapter 2, 51
Chapter 3, 107
Chapter 4, 138
Chapter 5, 198
Time considerations, 117, 121

Vacillation, 15

Written objectives, 77, 79

TUTORTEXTS

ADVANCED BIDDING by Charles H. Goren

ADVENTURES IN ALGEBRA by Norman A. Crowder and
    Grace C. Martin

THE AMERICAN CONSTITUTION by Gerald Leinwand

THE ARITHMETIC OF COMPUTERS by Norman A. Crowder

BASIC COMPUTER PROGRAMMING by Theodore G. Scott

BETTER BUSINESS ORGANIZATION by Neely D. Gardner

BUSINESS LETTER WRITING by James L. Slattery

COMPUTER PROGRAMMING TECHNIQUES by Theodore G. Scott

DECIMALS AND PERCENTAGE by Betty K. Friel

EFFECTIVE EXECUTIVE PRACTICES by Neely D. Gardner

EFFECTIVE WRITING by Kellog Smith and
    Jane Staple Ford

ELECTRON TUBES AT WORK by James B. Owens and
    Paul Sanborn

THE ELEMENTS OF BRIDGE by Charles H. Goren

FRACTIONS: A Basic Course in Arithmetic by Betty K. Friel

FUNDAMENTALS OF ELECTRICITY by James B. Owens and
    Paul Sanborn

INTRODUCTION TO ELECTRONICS by Robert J. Hughes and
    Peter Pipe

THE MEANING OF MODERN POETRY by John Clark Pratt

PARLIAMENTARY PROCEDURE by Warren Lehman

PRACTICAL LAW: A Course in Everyday Contracts
    by Warren Lehman

PRACTICAL MATHEMATICS by Grace C. Martin and Ann Smalley

PROPER PUNCTUATION by Kellog Smith and Leighton Steele

THE SLIDE RULE by Robert Saffold and Ann Smalley

TRIGONOMETRY: A Practical Course by Norman A. Crowder and Grace C. Martin

UNDERSTANDING SHAKESPEARE: Macbeth by Ruth Frieman

UNDERSTANDING STOCKS by Don G. Campbell

YOUR LIFE INSURANCE by Barbara H. Hathaway

G14